Retelling t.. ...

Retelling the Tale

An Introduction to
Medieval French Literature

Simon Gaunt

Duckworth

First published in 2001 by
Gerald Duckworth & Co. Ltd.
61 Frith Street, London W1D 3JL
Tel: 020 7434 4242
Fax: 020 7434 4420
Email: enquiries@duckworth-publishers.co.uk
www.ducknet.co.uk

A catalogue record for this book is available
from the British Library

ISBN 0 7156 2925 5

Typeset by Derek Doyle & Associates, Liverpool
Printed in Great Britain by Booksprint

Contents

Author's note

This book is intended for students and general readers beginning their exploration of medieval French literature. I have consequently kept references to a minimum, and, wherever possible, I have used editions of texts that are readily available, which often means editions in paperback series such as *Lettres Gothiques*. When making suggestions for further reading, I have concentrated on accessible recent works in English, with just the occasional reference to essential works in French: there is, of course, also a large body of writing on medieval French literature in German and Italian. Page references to secondary works are given only for quotations; otherwise the relevant section is easily located by consulting the index of the work in question. As it has not been my intention to write a conventional literary history of medieval France, I have not given precise dates in my text. I include a chronological table to help orient readers, along with a glossary of terms relevant to the study of Old French literature and a list of major authors and texts.

Acknowledgements

I should like to thank first and foremost Nick Hammond for asking me to write this book, for his helpful comments on my various drafts, and for his seemingly boundless cheerfulness and enthusiasm. I am no less warmly grateful to Elizabeth Edwards, Karen Pratt, Kathryn Robson and Mark Treharne, who, as interlocutors and as guinea-pig readers, curbed some of this book's excesses. They are by no means responsible for any remaining blunders or infelicities. I should like to dedicate this book to Kathryn, in every respect an ideal reader; also to the students in my first-year medieval literature class in King's College London during the 1999-2000 session, as their enthusiasm for Marie de France's *Lais* showed me yet again that some of these odd old stories still have something to say to us.

Simon Gaunt
London February 2001

Introduction

Medieval French Literature and the Voice in the Text

This is a book about story-telling. The stories that are told in medieval French texts for the first time include some of the most compelling of Western culture, ranging from the heroic deeds of the great warrior Roland, through the passionate love stories of Tristan and Yseult or Lancelot and Guinevere, to the arch and comic bawdy tales of the *fabliaux* or the *Roman de Renart*. I shall not attempt to offer a systematic literary history of medieval France. My intention is rather to offer an introduction to medieval French literature by inviting my readers to think about how to read a medieval narrative, about how it may or may not differ from a modern narrative, and about what preconceptions they may or may not bring to bear on what they read. My particular focus will be upon the role of reading and writing, since understanding the conditions in which medieval texts were produced, transmitted and received is crucial to understanding their narrative dynamic. I shall concentrate on medieval French literary texts written between 1100 and 1300, but before I turn to my main theme – reading and writing – I should first like to say a few words about my field of enquiry, 'medieval French literature', for however straightforward the meaning of these three terms may seem, each in fact raises a number of important preliminary problems that are worth articulating explicitly.

Literature

Very few texts in French survive from before 1100. This is not to say that people did not tell each other stories in French, or even write them down. But the paucity of examples of written French from before the twelfth century, particularly when compared with the volume of Latin texts that have survived, suggests French was over-

whelmingly an oral language. Written texts were therefore reserved
for the minority who could read and write Latin, that is clerics and
a few exceptional nobles. All this changes in the twelfth century: a
few texts in French composed before 1150 survive (though not necessarily in twelfth-century copies), but then after 1150 there seems
to have been an explosion of narratives in a variety of genres as well
as lyrics. By 1200 it is already possible to talk about a French literary
tradition, with authors recasting the material of their predecessors
and playing upon a knowledge of earlier texts. But we need to be
aware that the genres, forms, manner of composition and mode of
dissemination of medieval texts all differ markedly from those of
modern texts. Moreover, while the subject matter of some texts may
be familiar to some modern readers from modern adaptations, the
subject matter of many texts will seem strange, sometimes even out-
landish. To read a medieval narrative as if it were a modern novel
would clearly be a limiting and unsatisfactory experience, while to
spurn less familiar texts for apparently more straight-forward and
accessible tales of adventure and derring-do is to miss out on some
fabulously various, clever, often funny material. Indeed it is the
unfamiliarity of some medieval texts that can make them so
exciting and compelling.

In the Middle Ages there were a variety of distinct narrative
genres. The earliest narratives to have survived are saints' lives and
chansons de geste (heroic tales of knightly valour, often, but not
always, involving battles against the Saracen infidel). The mid
twelfth century sees the emergence of romance, tales of knightly
quests often involving a love intrigue and/or King Arthur and the
Knights of the Round Table. From the outset, the authors of French
literary texts seem to have had a propensity for humour, irony and
parody: in addition to parodic *chansons de geste* and romances, by
the end of the twelfth century two overtly comic, often bawdy,
genres are well established, the *fabliaux* (bawdy short stories) and
the parodic beast epic (or *Roman de Renart*). These different genres
distinguish themselves by their content, but also by their length and
form. Thus *chansons de geste* and romances vary enormously in
length from anything between 2000 and 20,000+ lines, but saints'
lives and *fabliaux* are usually much shorter as are the episodic

accounts of the misdeeds of Renart the wily fox and his beastly companions. Whereas *chansons de geste* and some early saints' lives are written in decasyllabic (i.e. the lines have 10 syllables) assonanced or rhyming stanzas of uneven length called *laisses*, most other texts are written in octosyllabic rhyming couplets (i.e. the lines have 8 syllables). As this implies, in the twelfth century most texts in French were composed in verse, but the early thirteenth century sees the adoption of prose, which was used in the twelfth century only for a few vernacular chronicles, for writing vast Arthurian romances (and chronicles). There were other innovations in the thirteenth century, such as the phenomenally successful allegorical romance the *Roman de la Rose* (on which see Chapter 5), but all the genres I have just briefly described, including the *chanson de geste*, continued to be vigorous through to the end of the century.

However different the form and content of these genres may be from modern narratives, the key difference lies in their manner of composition and mode of dissemination. Composed well before the invention of printing, and when modes of literacy were radically different, French texts from the twelfth and thirteenth centuries survive because they were written down, by hand, in manuscripts. As most texts from the period have features that suggest they were delivered orally and as some texts (for example *chansons de geste*) are thought by some to have been originally composed and disseminated orally, medieval French literature is often characterised as partaking of an oral culture. However, a clear-cut distinction between orality and writing is unhelpful. Because today we usually read silently, we tend to oppose the oral and the written, but this opposition does not hold for medieval culture. In this book, I wish to explore what distinguishes a manuscript from a print culture in order to bring into focus how the nature of medieval texts – medieval textuality – differs from that of modern texts, but in so doing I also hope to caution against any simplistic use of the notion of orality.

French

While it might have seemed obvious until comparatively recently to identify 'French literature' with France, recent interest in francophone literature from other parts of the world has problematised this equation of a nation state with a language and of both with a national literature. But the relationship between France, French as a language and 'French' literature was already complex in the Middle Ages. First, although the word 'France' was commonly used in many early texts, it did not mean what we understand by France today: at the beginning of the twelfth century, the king of France had direct control only of the area around Paris, known today as the Ile-de-France. Although most of the nobles who controlled the rest of France nominally owed allegiance to the king, in practice many could act independently, and frequently they did so to subvert his authority: there was no such thing as the modern entity known as France. Moreover, the French language was not spoken in vast areas of the territory we identify with France. Below a line a little to the south of the Loire, people spoke Occitan, an entirely separate romance language with its own lively literary culture (the troubadours), whereas other so-called regional languages (such as Breton, Walloon and Germanic dialects) hemmed French-speaking areas in far more tightly than they do today. French itself was a cluster of regional dialects (notably Picard, Champenois, Norman and so-called Francien, the dialect of Paris and the Ile-de-France). Most importantly of all, French was widely spoken in one important area outside modern France, England: many early medieval 'French' texts were in fact produced not in France, but in England or in parts of modern day France that were controlled by the English crown. Furthermore, because of political alliances and demographic movement engendered by the crusades, as a literary language French was used in courts as far afield as northern Italy and the Middle East.

Following the Norman invasion of England in 1066, a dialect of French (usually known as Anglo-Norman) became the language of the ruling classes in England until the later Middle Ages. Moreover, for a significant portion of the period covered by this book, extensive portions of the territory lying in present-day Western France had closer ties with England than with France. To understand why, one needs to have a sense of the marital manoeuvrings of the French and English royal families and the consequences these had for territorial allegiances. In 1137, Guilhem VIII Duke of Aquitaine died leaving his only daughter, Eleanor of Aquitaine, heiress to the County of Poitou and Duchy of Aquitaine and with a claim to the County of Toulouse. These territories made her potentially more powerful and certainly wealthier than the king of France, Louis VII, to whom she was betrothed and whom she duly married. But Eleanor, it would appear, was a headstrong and colourful character, while Louis was a mild, devout man who liked a quiet life: not only was their marriage apparently not a success, but crucially they failed to produce a male child. After some fairly torrid episodes of which we know only snippets, Eleanor left Louis in 1152 as he simultaneously divorced her (it is hard to tell which came first) and she instantly married one Henry Plantagenet, Count of Anjou, a move which can only have been calculated to annoy Louis, given the position of Henry's territory between Eleanor's and his own, and given also the vital consideration that Henry was heir (or pretender, depending on your point of view) to the English throne. Henry duly became King of England in 1154 and, to add insult to injury, he and Eleanor had 8 children, including 4 boys, Henry ('the Young King'), Richard (the Lionheart), Geoffrey (of Brittany) and John (Lackland, the prince John of the Robin Hood stories). Henry and Eleanor's marriage was stormy: he had her imprisoned for 11 years after she colluded with her sons in rebellion against him. But the power base it created was something of a medieval superpower, which was crucial to the growth of literacy in Western Europe in the twelfth century and to the development of 'French' literature: a fair number of the writers whose work will be discussed in this book lived in territories controlled by the Plantagenets, not in 'France' at all.

Medieval

In some senses what we mean by 'medieval' is obvious: the medieval period runs between the so-called 'Dark Ages' that followed the Roman Empire and the Renaissance. French specialists generally refer to the period before 1100 as the early Middle Ages, to the period that concerns this book as the 'high Middle Ages' (*le haut moyen âge*), and to the period between about 1300 and 1500 as the later Middle Ages: the French language in the last two of these three periods is usually referred to as 'Old' and 'Middle' French respectively.

The problem is that the adjective 'medieval' sometimes implies an understanding of history that is questionable; moreover it has a number of meanings in popular usage that are equally questionable. In recent years (particularly since the work of Mikail Bakhtin and Michel Foucault), it has become fashionable to offer an account of European culture and history that stresses the importance of the early modern period in the evolution of our own cultural identities. Classical Greece and Rome are construed as radically different from modern culture and it was the rediscovery of this otherness in the so-called Renaissance along with economic developments (a monetary economy), technological breakthroughs (printing), theological shifts (the Reformation), literary triumphs (the novel) and geographical 'discoveries' (America) that produced the conditions that made the evolution of modern European cultures – with their apparently unique complex subjectivities – possible. According to this account, the Middle Ages are simply what lies between what matters, literally in the middle, alternately represented as an age of primitive, unsophisticated and aggressive cultural floundering or of naïve idealism. Hence, there are two pejorative meanings of the adjective 'medieval' in common usage: excessive cruelty or violence is frequently described as 'medieval'; as is something innocent, quaint or with twee olde worlde or fantastic qualities such as a 'medieval' banquet or some children's books (such as *The Hobbit*).

Of course the early modern period *is* different from the Middle Ages, but the constant attention historians and literary or cultural critics pay to what they see as the rupture caused by the invention of printing, the Reformation, the 'discovery' of America, and so on, can blind us to the historical continuity that links the medieval, the early modern and the modern periods. For example, an embryonic monetary economy is discernible in the twelfth century, while the religious issues that split Europe in two during the Reformation (such as worshipping images, or the sanctity of marriage) were already deeply controversial throughout the Middle

Ages. Of course, printing represents an important technological advance in Europe at the end of the fifteenth century, but it often goes unremarked that the voracious demand for books that printing satisfied had been engendered by growing literacy rates and a dramatic increase in the demand for texts that can be traced back to the twelfth century.

The Renaissance, far from being simply the dramatic rupture in European cultural history that some early modernists and modernists frequently take it to have been, owed a good deal to the period that preceded it. In particular, the twelfth and thirteenth centuries were extraordinary rich in cultural achievements. This was the period when the great Romanesque and Gothic cathedrals were constructed, when Western Europe came dramatically into contact with other cultures through the Crusades, when vernacular literature was born, and when a new psycho-sexual dynamic that became the foundation of modern sexual identities emerged in the aristocratic courts of France and Occitania, what we now call 'courtly love'. Moreover, the first universities were founded in this period and from these emerged extraordinary powerful thinkers such as Abelard, Thomas Aquinas and vernacular writers of equal sophistication like Jean de Meun. In addition, the origins of modern European states, with their complex machinery of government, are to be found in the twelfth century, while the great monarchies of the early modern period (for example France, Spain and England) or other institutions of government such as the Papacy, the Italian city states and German principalities, survived basically in their medieval form. The 'medieval' period had a complex, dazzling and sophisticated culture, so to imply it is naïve or primitive is disingenuous to say the least.

It is similarly disingenuous to describe excessive violence or callous barbarism as 'medieval'. Can an age that gave the world nuclear weapons and concentration camps, or baptised routine massacres with the euphemistic term 'ethnic cleansing' really, in all conscience, castigate another period for its violent tendencies? We are inclined, as many cultural critics have pointed out, to project on to other cultures our own blind spots and difficulties. This is not to say that the Middle Ages were not violent. But they were no more violent or barbaric than any other period in history and the technology of killing certainly meant that the scale of violence was less than today. Furthermore, sensibilities were undoubtedly different. For example, it may well be the case that people living in a medieval town in France would have witnessed public executions that would make our stomachs turn, but I imagine that these same medieval people would have been horrified at the idea that anyone might watch movies like *The Exorcist* or *American Psycho* as entertainment. And public executions are by no means a thing of the distant past, even in Europe or the US.

So when we read 'medieval' 'French' 'literature' we should not impose modern notions of what constitutes the medieval, Frenchness or the literary upon texts from this distant past; we also need, of course, to be alert to medieval French literature's cultural specificity. I shall devote the remainder of this introduction to a sketch of medieval orality and literacy with a view, then, to suggesting how this might inform our reading of texts.

Orality and literacy in twelfth- and thirteenth-century France

Levels of literacy were generally low and whereas today it is assumed that one must be able to read and write in order to occupy a position of authority, this was not necessarily the case in the twelfth century. Reading and, as we will see, particularly writing were largely the preserve of the clergy, or more precisely, the clerisy, that is to say clerks, and although very rarely some people may have learnt to read and write solely through the medium of the vernacular, the overwhelming majority of literate men (and the overwhelming majority of literate people were men) had learnt to read and write through the medium of Latin. Clerks were men who had taken preliminary vows and had themselves tonsured (had the top of their heads shaved as a sign of their clerical status): this might mean that they intended to become priests or monks, but it might simply mean that they were receiving, or had received, some minimal education in a church school (possibly with a view to finding employment). Although being a clerk was supposedly a sign of literacy, the reading skills of many clerks were notoriously poor. Moreover, reading and writing were two separate activities in the Middle Ages, with more people being able to read than write. Before the widespread use of paper (which is an easy surface to write upon), texts had to be copied laboriously on parchment, which was not only expensive, but difficult to work with. So as not to waste precious parchment, rough drafts were produced on wax tablets or (more commonly it is believed) texts were composed through dictation to professional scribes who had been trained to write neatly and legibly: most people did not have the patience or the skill to write consistently in a sufficiently legible manner. The cost of the material, the cost of labour, and the complex assembly of a book meant that manuscripts were luxury items, reserved for the wealthy.

Ordinary people may have felt alienated from writing in a number of ways. Firstly and most obviously, they were unable to read. Secondly, the majority of texts were written in Latin, so even if they were read aloud many did not understand them. Thirdly, writing was associated with clerks and churchman. Finally, writing may not always have been trusted. Thus, it is sometimes argued that a written document was not necessarily trustworthy evidence of a land transaction, that vast areas of Europe were more influenced by customary law (transmitted orally) than by written legal codes, and that an eye-witness was intrinsically more believable than documentary evidence. Moreover, the nobility, supposedly the patrons and main public of many vernacular literary texts, sometimes seemed to value the skills associated with knighthood more than the skills associated with book-learning. This is reflected in the traditional opposition that is made in many texts between *chevalerie* (knightly skills) and *clergie* (clerkly skills), which is formalised in debate poems about who makes the better lover: a knight or a clerk?

Scholars are by no means unanimous in their view of the status of writing in the production, dissemination and reception of medieval French literature. If some stress the centrality of *clergie* – and therefore of writing – others argue that as modern readers we need to be wary of reading these texts as if they were modern written texts, intended to be *read*, for they were in fact intended to be *heard*, and not just heard as someone read a fixed text aloud, but heard as someone performed the text, enhancing the words with gestures, tone of voice, mimicry and so on. Moreover, for the more ardent proponents of orality, medieval French literary texts at least in the earliest period (that is before 1200) were not (or rarely) committed to writing at all: they were composed, performed and transmitted to new performers orally. According to this view, to interact with them as written texts is to miss something fundamental about their aesthetic. For such critics modern culture is so biased in favour of writing that it is unable to appreciate fully the aesthetic grandeur of some of these oral texts *as oral texts* (see, for example, Vitz and Zumthor).

Orality is thought to be particularly central to the *chansons de geste*, to other genres that apparently express a communal ideology, such as saints' lives, or to genres such as *lais* that refer to oral sources. According to the twelfth-century chroniclers William of Malmesbury and Wace, a minstrel performed a version of the *Chanson de Roland* before the Battle of Hastings to encourage the Norman troops. Few scholars today take this assertion at face value, yet the image of the story-teller / singer of tales rousing his audience by engaging them orally, without the aid of a written text, is an enduring one. It is part of a nostalgic vision of an heroic by-gone age when life was at one and the same time more straightforward and yet also more exhilarating. This vision still appeals to many. Thus, Evelyn Birge Vitz has recently made the case for oral – and textless – composition and dissemination of romance.

However, the importance of writing in the evolution of medieval vernacular culture, and indeed the growing role of literacy in society as a whole, should not be underestimated, while 'orality', at least as it emerges from surviving literary texts, can by no means simply be opposed straightforwardly to writing.

Research by cultural historians over the last few decades suggests that there was a marked increase in the use of writing and in literacy in the twelfth century, particularly in the second half of the century, which is the period when we see an explosion of vernacular literary activity in French-speaking and other areas of

Europe, a coincidence that is hard to ignore. The larger, more powerful and increasingly centralised kingdom of Henry II in England, with its vast areas of dependent territories on the continent, needed ever more elaborate administrative structures in order to keep track of financial matters, property transactions and day-to-day affairs of government. Largely in response to Henry II's formidable power-base on his western flank, Louis VII's son and heir, Philippe-Auguste, sought to strengthen the position of the French monarchy and as he did so, he too set new administrative structures in place. These developments should not be exaggerated, for we are by no means talking about a fully-fledged bureaucracy, but, as Michael Clanchy has shown in his aptly titled *From Memory to Written Record*, the twelfth century sees the beginning of a dramatic increase in the production of documents pertaining to land transactions, finances and so on. As more documents began to be produced and circulated, more people needed to be able to read and it became hard to function effectively in many areas of public life unless one had at least some rudimentary literacy. Until the twelfth century, reading and writing were largely the preserve of the clergy. By 1200 royal courts, and some other less exalted courts, had organised writing offices for the production of documents. Anyone who dealt with these embryonic administrative structures needed some kind of literacy.

The growth of a literate laity in Western Europe was largely pragmatic. It was not necessarily driven by a thirst for learning or the pleasures of literature. But as more people learned to read, the public for written texts increased. Although as a general rule it is probably true to say that many noble men and the vast majority of women or peasants could still not read, exceptions are numerous and there is evidence that significant numbers of knights, non-noble boys and even a few women learnt to read from clerks, local priests, parents. Indeed the reading public became relatively heterogeneous and, as we will see, characters in texts are frequently represented as being able to read, or at the very least as using texts in order to pursue their lives.

This last point is important, for in a number of respects it is crucial not to stress unduly the ability to read since the key issue is

whether written texts are important to twelfth- and thirteenth-
century French culture, whether, in other words, we are dealing with
what might be described as a textual culture. The shift that Clanchy
charts in *From Memory to Written Record* does not simply concern an
increase in a learned skill, it concerns more importantly a shift in
mentality to a culture in which the written record is seen as inherently more reliable and trustworthy than memory or oral witness.
The growth of a textual culture is not simply the result of more individuals being able to read and write, it is a consequence of writing
and therefore written texts being valued as a source of knowledge,
whether this be collective or individual wisdom. In *The Implications of
Literacy* and *Listening for the Text*, Brian Stock argues that the key development in twelfth-century Europe was less the growth of literacy *per
se*, which in any case never led to anything like what we would regard
as a literate society, than the growing reliance on texts as a source of
authority and knowledge, as a forum for debate. Put simply, it is a
question of primacy. Which is culturally more important, the spoken
or the written word? What Clanchy, Stock and others show is that
there is a growing tendency, from the twelfth century onwards, to
privilege the written over the spoken word and, as we will see, the
centrality of writing in medieval French culture is something that
emerges clearly from medieval French literary texts. This shift in
mentality that is marked by the importance accorded to writing in
the twelfth century reflects in many important respects the insight of
the modern philosopher Jacques Derrida in his famous early work, *De
la Grammatologie*: once writing has become central to a culture, it
informs the way in which *everyone* uses language – including those
who cannot read or write – because it brings everyone into contact
with a radically different way of using language. Writing introduces a
model of language grounded in the absence of a speaker and therefore in displacement and deferral (as opposed to a model that
necessarily relies on a speaker's presence). As we will see, this insight
is important to an understanding of medieval French literature.

But as I have already suggested, reading and writing in the
twelfth century did not necessarily mean the same thing as they do
now. As Dennis Green succinctly puts it, 'reading was an intellectual attainment (no matter how elementary), whilst writing was

more a manual skill and formed no part of the discipline of letters' (*Medieval Listening*, p. 9). Moreover, many people who could read may well not have been able to read silently, even though silent reading may not have been as unusual in the Middle Ages as has often been thought. In his *Confessions*, which were widely disseminated in the Middle Ages, the great fourth-century theologian Augustine famously marvels at the ability of his teacher and mentor, Ambrose, to read silently and throughout the Middle Ages when someone is able to read silently, this is usually remarked upon with some astonishment, in terms that echo Augustine. In his ground-breaking and still important study *From Script to Print*, H.J. Chaytor argued that silent reading was facilitated by the technological breakthrough of printing. Before the invention of printing, there were no fixed rules for spelling or word division, which might vary widely even in the work of a single scribe in a single text. Chaytor thought that all texts were deciphered by a process of voicing the words out loud so that even when copying a text, a scribe read every word aloud and then wrote down what he heard, rather than copying what he read in his original. But recently Paul Saenger has shown that silent reading was in fact more common than had previously been thought in the Middle Ages, with the general growth of literacy that takes place in the twelfth century being paralleled by a concomitant growth in silent reading. Evidence from some manuscripts, where we have two copies of a single source, suggests that scribes were sometimes at least copying what they *saw*, rather than what they *heard* as a result of reading what they saw: they became far more like modern typists – quite capable of copying a model accurately without understanding it. This again points to a shift towards a mentality in which the written word is becoming more important than the spoken word.

Silent reading has a profound impact on how people view texts. When read silently, a text is an object of silent and individual contemplation rather than a communal and shared experience. Silent reading has a significant impact on how we think about individuality and privacy since it makes it possible to communicate with the past through texts *by oneself* and radically enhances the extent to which one's spiritual development may be internalised, no one else's business but one's own. Compare, for example, a culture in which one only ever hears the Bible read aloud by someone else, who chooses the extracts and inflects them with his or her own tone of voice, to a culture in which one may contemplate and reread passages at one's leisure. In the twelfth century spaces for private reading start to be built in monasteries, a sign that the nature of interaction with texts was changing.

Having said this, there can be no doubt that most texts continued to be read aloud throughout the Middle Ages. But if some people could read silently, presumably others could learn the skill and it may well be the case (as Joyce Coleman has suggested for the later medieval period in England) that literary texts were often read aloud because this is what people preferred. That texts were read aloud is unquestionable from references in a wide range of texts. Many of these references make it clear that we are dealing with a written text intended for public reading:

> Qui l'estoire savoir voldra
> Lise le Brut, illoc l'orra.
> (*Histoire de Weldef*, quoted in Clanchy, p. 216)

(Let whoever wants to know this story read the *Brut* and he will hear it there.)

> Seignurs, oi avez le vers del parchemin
> Cum li bers Aaluf est venuz a sa fin.
> (*Roman de Horn*, quoted in Chaytor, p. 12)

(My lords, you have heard the verse from the parchment relating how sir Aaluf met his end.)

But if texts were intended to be read aloud, we should be wary of assuming therefore that they were composed exclusively with public reading in mind, and, as Dennis Green argues throughout his important study of orality and writing in medieval German culture, many authors composed with a dual public of silent readers and public auditors in mind. A corollary of this, as Green contends, is that oral and written culture in fact interpenetrate each other deeply in medieval culture, which has a profound impact on the style and rhetoric of medieval texts. As we can see from the two examples I have just quoted, a written text will often assume an *audience* of *listeners* while nonetheless signalling the presence of a book. A direct address to an audience, the use of verbs like 'to hear', 'to say' or 'to listen' cannot therefore be taken as evidence that a written text is simply a reflection of an originally text-less performance, of a text's orality. These features of Old French rhetoric do, however, call attention to a fundamental flaw in any straightforward opposition of orality to writing: written texts are always to a certain extent conceived as 'voiced' in the Middle Ages because they were usually read aloud. In any case, as we will see, Old French texts evince a strong awareness of the value and uses of writing: when they evoke oral story-telling they do so from within a culture for which writing is already crucial.

In order to understand the dynamics of medieval story-telling we need, then, to be wary of making straightforward assumptions about the ostensible orality of medieval texts. If, as we will see, these texts appeal to the oral, they do so from within a culture that is already clearly imbued with the importance of writing. In Chapter 1, I will analyse the effect of 'oral' style in one well-known written text, the *Chanson de Roland*. The complex interplay between orality and writing and how this impacts upon story-telling will be the subject of Chapters 2 and 3. The way the integrity of the text itself and the status of the author are problematised in medieval French texts by the manuscript culture that produces them will be examined in Chapters 4 and 5. Chapters 6 and 7 will be devoted to the phenomenon that gives this book its main title: *retelling the tale*, that is the medieval proclivity for reworking existing texts to give them new life and new interpretations, thereby engendering a culture profoundly interested in interpretation, debate, and intellectual enquiry.

Given the constraints on space in a book of this kind, I have made no attempt to offer comprehensive coverage of twelfth- and

thirteenth-century French texts: I particularly regret that it has not
been possible to include discussion of the *fabliaux*, of lyric poetry,
or of romances with interpolated lyrics.

Selected Reading

Henry J. Chaytor, *From Script to Print: An Introduction to Medieval Vernacular
    Literature* (Cambridge, 1945). Classic account of medieval textuality.
M.T. Clanchy, *From Memory to Written Record: England 1066-1307* (London,
    1979). Brilliant account of the importance of writing after 1100.
Joyce Coleman, *Public Reading and the Reading Public in Late Medieval
    Engand and France* (Cambridge, 1996). Mainly on later medieval
    England, but relevant to twelfth-century France.
Jacques Derrida, *De la Grammatologie* (Paris, 1967). Influential philosoph-
    ical essay on the nature of language, both written and spoken. Not for
    the faint-hearted.
Dennis H. Green, *Medieval Listening and Reading: The Primary Reception of
    German Literature 800-1300* (Cambridge, 1994). Account of medieval
    textuality in Germany, but relevant to France. Scholarly and dense.
Walter J. Ong, *Orality and Literacy: the Technologizing of the Word* (London
    and NY, 1982). Typical of the work of this writer who influences Vitz
    and Zumthor.
M.B. Parkes, 'The literacy of the laity', in *Literature and Western Civilization:
    The Medieval World*, ed. D. Daiches and A. Thorlby, 6 vols (London,
    1973), II, pp. 555-77. Excellent overview.
Paul Saenger, *Space Between Words: the Origin of Silent Reading* (Stanford,
    1997). Strictly for the bookish.
Brian Stock, *The Implications of Literacy: Written Language and Models of
    Interpretation in the Eleventh and Twelfth Centuries* (Princeton, 1983). A
    demanding, but rewarding read.
—————— *Listening for the Text: on the Uses of the Past* (Philadelphia, 1996). An
    accessible collection of Stock's essays.
Evelyn Birge Vitz, *Orality and Performance in Early French Romance*
    (Woodbridge, 1999). Puts the case for the 'orality' of medieval French
    literature polemically.
Paul Zumthor, *La Poésie et la voix dans la civilisation médiévale* (Paris, 1984).
    Good example of the work of one of the most influential medievalists
    of the post-war period. Puts the case for the 'orality' of medieval French
    literature strongly.

1

The Oxford *Roland*'s 'Oral' Style

Let us now take a closer look at a text that is often taken as exemplary of twelfth-century French culture's supposed orality: the Oxford version of the *Chanson de Roland*. What are the stylistic features that have been taken as indices of its orality? What does a text like this say about writing?

The Oxford *Roland* is generally acknowledged as one of the greatest and most powerful texts in the Old French canon. Composed most probably in the second half of the eleventh century in an Anglo-Norman dialect, it numbers among the earliest surviving literary texts in French, while the manuscript in which it has been preserved (which is now kept in Oxford, hence the 'Oxford *Roland*') probably dates from between 1140 and 1170. This makes the Oxford *Roland* doubly precocious: not only is it an unusually early text (the overwhelming majority of the 120 or so surviving *chansons de geste* date from after 1150), it also survives in an unusually early manuscript (most literary texts composed in the twelfth century survive in manuscripts dating from the thirteenth). It is referred to as the Oxford *Roland* to distinguish it from other versions of the same poem, later adaptations of a text that must have been very like the Oxford *Roland* even if they did not derive from precisely the copy that has come down to us. (I shall comment on one of these other versions in Chapter 6.) These later adaptations are generally treated with scorn by modern critics. They are thought to be but pale reflections of the original masterpiece, which is instructive as to the differences between medieval and modern attitudes towards texts. As we will see, whereas adapting, expanding, *rewriting* texts is characteristic of medieval culture, today we tend to regard what the 'original' author wrote as sacred, inviolable, inherently more worthy than a text that has undergone reworking at the hands of others. The Oxford *Roland* has a unique status in modern views of medieval French culture: it is often one of the first texts studied in university courses and it is sometimes cited as the purest form of medieval French epic composition. And yet other versions of the *Roland* were better known in the Middle Ages and, although it is sometimes taken as the bench-mark of epic style, the Oxford Roland's style is unusually mannered and in fact atypical of the genre as a whole. This style is often portrayed as quintessentially oral, which is not to say that it is taken for granted that the Oxford *Roland* derives from an orally transmitted poem (though this is the view of some scholars), but rather that its main stylistic features are redolent of orality.

The *Chanson de Roland* tells the story of a disastrous French defeat at Roncevaux in the Pyrenees as Charlemagne's army returns from a victorious Spanish campaign. The historical battle commemorated in the poem took place in 778, but it was actually the Basques rather than the Saracens who ambushed the French rear-guard and this historical inaccuracy is sometimes attributed to the story having been handed down orally from the eighth to the eleventh centuries. In the poem, the fiery and impetuous hero Roland, who is Charlemagne's nephew and favourite, has an angry confrontation with his step-father Ganelon over the strategy the conquering army should adopt as it returns home. As a result, Ganelon is sent on an embassy to the Saracen camp which he uses as a means of betraying Roland, who is left in the rear-guard as Charlemagne's army crosses the Pyrenees. A mighty battle leaves the rear-guard massacred, including Roland and his beloved companion Oliver. But Charlemagne returns to inflict an awesome defeat on the Saracens in revenge for the loss of his favourite. In the final scenes Ganelon is punished for his treachery and Charlemagne lives to fight – wearily – another day.

The poem is an elegiac celebration of bravery and warfare. Violence is described with lyrical beauty as thousands of men get chopped to pieces, dismembered and disembowelled. The lyricism derives from dense patterns of repetition within and between *laisses* – the assonanced or sometimes rhymed stanzas of unequal length in which *chansons de geste* are composed – and these patterns are thought to be clear indices of the poem being intended for oral delivery, given their poetic effects and the occurrence of similar patterns of repetition in oral traditions of epic poetry throughout the world. Perhaps the most famous examples of this style occur in the two so-called horn scenes. In the first, realising they have been tricked and are surrounded by Saracens, Oliver, who is a sensible strategist, urges Roland to blow his renowned Olifant (a sort of horn) to summon Charlemagne back to help them: Roland refuses as he claims this will mean losing face. Then, towards the end of the battle, Roland, in an apparent change of heart, declares he will blow his horn to summon Charlemagne back to take revenge for their by now inevitable deaths: Oliver is adamant that he should not do this as it would be shameful to call for help once the battle has started. Their dialogue in these scenes records a conflict of values (honour vs. pragmatism) that critics have been debating hotly since the *Roland* first became the object of literary criticism in the nineteenth century. But the values endorsed by the text would seem to be Roland's since, as we all know, he blows the horn and the rest of the poem, its tragedy, is *his* story, not Oliver's. In each of the horn scenes the characters' exchange is repeated lyrically three times, each time with subtle differences, to produce a powerfully intense moment.

To give a sense of how this manner of using repetition works to extraordinary lyrical effect, I have chosen to examine not the horn scenes, since they are so well-known, but the equally beautiful and powerful moment when the dying Roland tries to break his beloved sword Durendal so that it does not fall into Saracen hands:

171

Ço sent Rollant la veüe ad perdue,
Met sei sur piez, quanqu'il poet s'esvertüet;
En sun visage sa culur ad perdue.
Dedevant lui une perre ad veüe: 2300
Dis colps i fiert par doel e par rancune;
Cruist li acers, ne freint ne ne s'esgruignet.

'Eh!', dist li quens, 'seinte Marie, aiüe!
E! Durendal, bone, si mare fustes!
Quant jo mei perd, de vos nen ai mais cure.   2305
Tantes batailles en camp en ai vencues
E tantes teres larges escumbatues
Que Carles tient ki la barbe ad canue!
Ne vos ait hume ki pur altre s'en fuiet!
Mult bon vassal vos ad lung tens tenue;   2310
Jamais n'ert tel en France l'asolue.'

172

Rollant ferit el perrun de sardanie:
Cruist li acers, ne briset ne n'esgranie.
Quant il ço vit que n'en pout mie freindre,
A sei meïsme la cumencet a pleindre: 2315
'E! Durendal, cum es e clere e blanche!
Cuntre soleill si luises e reflambes!
Carles esteit es vals de Morïane,
Quant Deus del cel li mandat par sun angle
Qu'il te dunast a un cunte cataignie;   2320
Dunc la me ceinst li gentilz reis, li magnes.
Jo l'en cunquis e Anjou e Bretaigne,
Si l'en cunquis e Peitou e le Maine;
Jo l'en cunquis Normendie la franche,
Si l'en cunquis Provence e Equitaigne   2325
E Lumbardie e trestute Romaine,
Jo l'en cunquis Baiver e tute Flandres
E Buguerie e trestute Puillanie,
Costentinnoble, dunt il out la fiance,
E en Saisonie fait il ço qu'il demandet;   2330
Jo l'en cunquis e Escoce e Irlande,
E Engletere, quë il teneit sa cambre;
Cunquis l'en ai païs e teres tantes,
Que Carles tient ki ad la barbe blanche.
Pur ceste espee ai dulor e pesance: 2335
Mielz voeill murir qu'entre paiens remaigne;
Damnesdeus perre, n'en laiser hunir France.

173

Rollant ferit en une perre bise,
Plus en abat que jo ne vos sai dire.
L'espee cruist, ne fruisset ne ne brise,   2340
Cuntre le ciel amunt est resortie.
Quant veit li quens que ne la freindrat mie,
Mult dulcement la pleinst a sei meïsme:
'E! Durendal, cum es bele e seintisme!
En l'oriét punt asez i ad reliques: 2345
La dent seint Perre e del sanc seint Basilie
E des chevels mun seignor seint Denise,
Del vestement i ad seinte Marie.
Il nen est dreiz que paiens te baillisent;
De crestïens devez estre servie.   2350
Ne vos ait hume ki facet cuardie!
Mult larges teres de vus avrai cunquises,
Que Carles tient ki la barbe ad flurie;
Li empereres en est e ber e riches.'

(Roland senses that he has lost his sight, he stands up and
musters as much strength as he can; the colour has drained
from his face. He has seen a rock before him: he strikes it ten
times full of sorrow and rancour; the steel clatters, but it neither breaks nor splinters. 'Alas!', says the count, 'Holy Mary,
help me! Alas, sturdy Durendal that you ever existed. Since I
am dying, I no longer have use for you. I have been victorious
on so many battlefields and conquered so many vast lands
that white-bearded Charles now controls! Let no man who
flees on account of another man ever possess you. A very
brave knight has held you for a good long time: holy France
will never see his like again!'

Roland struck on the sardonyx stone: the steel clatters, but
it neither smashes nor splinters. When he sees that he cannot
break it, he begins to lament to himself: 'Alas! Durendal, how
brilliant and bright you are! You shine and glitter in the sun!
Charles was in the valleys of Maurienne when God sent word
by his angel from heaven that he should give you to a warrior

count; and so that noble and great king girded me with it. I conquered with it Anjou and Brittany for him and I conquered with it Poitou and Maine for him; I conquered with it Normandy the free for him and I conquered with it Provence and Aquitaine for him, and Lombardy and all the area around Rome, I conquered with it Bavaria and all of Flanders for him and Bulgaria and all of Poland, Constantinople, from which he received a pledge of faith, and in Saxony he commands as he wills; I conquered with it Scotland and Ireland for him, and England, which he had as his own private property; I conquered with it so many countries and lands that white-bearded Charles now controls. I have great pain and sorrow on account of this sword: I would rather die than see it remain among Saracens; God, our Father, spare France this shame!'

Roland struck down on the solid rock harder than I can tell you. The sword clatters, but it neither splinters nor breaks, but instead it bounces back up towards the sky. When the count sees that he will not succeed in breaking it, he laments softly to himself: 'Alas, Durendal, how fair and holy you are! In your golden hilt are many relics. There is a tooth of Saint Peter and a drop of Saint Basil's blood and some hairs from my lord Saint Denis's head and a piece of holy Mary's clothing. It is not right that Saracens should take you; you should be served by Christians. The man who wields you should be no coward! I shall have conquered with you vast lands that white-bearded Charles controls; the Emperor is strong and powerful because of this.')

The style of an extract like this is frequently described as formulaic, by which is meant the frequent repeated use of chunks of texts that fit the metre of poem. Thus 'Rollant ferit' (lines 2312 and 2338), 'Cruist li acers' (lines 2302 and 2313) and 'E! Durendal ...' (lines 2304, 2316 and 2344) each consist of four syllables and therefore fit perfectly the first hemistich (or part) of an epic line, which conventionally may have a pause (known as a caesura) after four syllables. In *laisse* 172, 'Jo l'en cunquis' / 'Si l'en cunquis' represents a similarly handy rhythmic filler and formulae such as these, or tags such as 'ki la barbe ad canue/ blanche/ flurie!' (lines 2308, 2334, 2353) are thought to be the stock in trade of the oral poet, who draws on such formulae as he *recomposes* the poem orally with a degree of improvisation. Also redolent of oral poetry is the switching of tenses, which can serve to intensify the action or quicken the pace as one gets the impression that things are happening so fast that the speaker cannot keep pace with them.

The grandeur of this moment is extraordinary. Durendal glitters in the sun as the dying Roland, mustering all his prodigious strength, fails to break it, thereby symbolically marking the indestructibility of his own valiant will. But the effects of this extract are by no means straightforward. The repetition of *laisses*, which are called *laisses similaires* because the same thing is narrated more than once in similar, but slightly different terms, have similar effects to the use of slow motion to repeat an action in a movie. Are we supposed to think that Roland in fact laments after he has failed to shatter Durendal three times? Or should we see each stanza as a slightly different take on the same action? Similarly: did Oliver ask Roland to blow the horn three times or are we given three different takes on this? And then did Oliver try to stop him blowing the horn three times in the second horn scene, or are we given three different ways of viewing Oliver's resistance to blowing the horn once the battle has started? As in the *laisses similaires* of the horn scenes, each of the three *laisses* here stresses a different element of Roland's heroism: *laisse* 171 stresses his personal valour (see particularly line 2310), *laisse* 172 his service to Charlemagne pointedly rendered through the extended list of all his conquests, and *laisse* 173 his service to God, symbolised by the holy relics in Durendal's hilt. Each of Roland's laments invests Durendal – the symbol of his worth – with added meaning. But what are we to make of this layering? Does he move from the least to the most important element? Or conversely, does he start with what he regards as essential and then give it added value by supplementing it with patriotism and godliness?

Formulaic style leads to fundamental ambiguity here. Even when heard rather than read, a passage such as this constitutes an

interpretative challenge to the audience, inviting it to think about
what is going on, or even perhaps (implicitly) to *debate* the relative
merits of the values Roland evokes, since these are by no means
compatible with each other, as Oliver has been at pains to point
out ('Vostre proëcce Rollant, mar la veïmes', line 1731: I rue the
day we encountered your bravery, Roland). While there can be no
doubt that the text foregrounds Roland, celebrating his impetu-
osity as a virtue, the fact that there are counter voices *within* the
text shows the extent to which it acknowledges the complexity of
the issues at stake.

How 'oral' then is the formulaic style? As many critics have
pointed out, writers are quite capable of adopting stylistic features
that are associated with oral poetry: think of the novels of
Marguerite Duras or Salman Rushdie. In any case, if there can be
no doubt that the style of the Oxford *Roland* owes much to the style
of contemporary oral story telling (as do *L'Amant* or *Midnight's
Children*), as soon as it is written down (and we know that it was
written down even in the twelfth century) it becomes a *representation* of an oral text and is no longer an oral text itself. As far as we,
as modern readers, are concerned, text precedes voice, the written
word is primary, it evokes a voice but is not necessarily a faithful
record of a performance.

Why is it important to realise this?

If one views texts such as these as primarily oral, one can quickly
come to disregard the text we know in favour of a supposed absent
'original' from which it derives. As Brian Stock astutely puts it,
medieval epics '... do not recall a living "oral" society, but rather
the conventions through which its literary subjects sought to
render it for posterity' (*Implications*, p. 33). The medieval epics we
know are *written* texts. We may quite like to know about the oral
poems that may or may not have preceded them, but we cannot.
This does not make the written poems we do have less worthy as
object of study *as written poems*. Attention to the orality of medieval
texts leads some modern critics to see the voice as the only guar-
antor of truth, purity and aesthetic plenitude, with the written texts
that they read offering but a vague simulacrum of this. Consider
the words of Paul Zumthor, one of the most influential and sophis-

ticated theorists of medieval orality: 'nos textes ne nous livrent qu'une forme vide et sans doute fort profondément altérée de ce qui fut, dans un autre contexte sensori-moteur, parole pleine' (*La Poésie*, p. 68: our texts can only provide us with an empty form that can undoubtedly be shown to be profoundly wanting when compared to what, in another physical context, was fully meaningful speech). According to Zumthor the written text 'acquiert un pouvoir d'abstraction, de réflexion sur soi ... qu'il n'avait pas en régime de libre oralité; la langue n'est plus tout à fait transparente' (p. 113: acquires a power of abstraction, of self-reflexivity ... that it did not possess in its truly oral stage; language is no longer totally transparent). But, as we have seen, a poem like the Oxford *Roland*, which for Zumthor would be an example of the 'régime de libre oralité' is neither unchallenging nor straightforward. It is highly reflexive. Zumthor's position is perhaps illuminated by Brian Stock's contention that 'studies of orality are sometimes nostalgic pleas on behalf of traditions that have disappeared or are threatened' (*Listening*, p. 9). The oral text that some believe preceded the Oxford *Roland* may or may not have existed, but it certainly no longer exists.

Of course, I am by no means the only person to have argued against a straightforward view of the orality of the *chansons de geste*. An important school of critics, following in the wake of the great French medievalist Joseph Bédier, argued that the *chansons de geste*, far from being the result of a popular, oral tradition, were written texts conceived as propaganda for monasteries and other notable places along the great pilgrim routes. Roncevaux, for example, was on the main pilgrim route from France to Santiago de Compostella. Thus great epic stories may have been drawn from popular legend, but they were committed to writing from the eleventh century onwards by clerics who were imitating a popular style while working with their own, largely political agenda. Whatever the origins of the *chanson de geste*, in the twelfth and thirteenth centuries it is a genre with a vibrant and dynamic written tradition.

One reflection of this written tradition is the existence of cyclic manuscripts. These are compilations of *chansons de geste* about a single character, or his offspring, so that they read as a continuous

narrative. The most common example of this kind of epic cycle is
the sequence of *chansons de geste* devoted to William of Orange,
some of which veer towards the comic. Unlike Roland, William
always seems to live to fight another day and he devotes much of
his life to supporting Charlemagne's weak, floundering and
unworthy son Louis before striking out in search of a fief as a consequence of Louis' failure to reward him for his loyalty and
prowess. Although the use that these texts make of formulaic style
is less intense and lyrical than that of the Oxford *Roland*, they
nonetheless have features which at first glance make them seem
more 'oral' rather than written. Here is the altogether typical
opening of a poem from this cycle:

> Oiez, seignor, que Deus vos seit aidanz!
> Plaist vos oïr d'une estoire vaillant
> Bone chançon, corteise et avenant?
> Vilains joglere ne sai por quei se vant
> Nul mot en die tresque on li comant.
> De Looïs ne lairai ne vos chant
> Et de Guillelme al Cort nés le vaillant,
> Que tant sofri sor sarrazine gent;
> Du meillor ome ne cuit que nuls vos chant.
>
> (*Couronnement*, 1-9)

(Listen, my lords, and may God help you! Would you like to
hear a good song that is courtly and seemly, relating a noble
story? I do not know why an unworthy minstrel boasts, for he
says nothing unless commanded to do so. I will not desist
from singing to you about Louis, and about brave William of
the Short Nose, who suffered so greatly at the hands of
Saracens; to my mind no one ever sung of a better man.)

The text enjoins one to listen and designates itself as a *chanson* to
be sung. But the epics in this cycle only survive in cyclical manuscripts that organise them as part of a chronological written
narrative. These manuscripts are often large-format, meticulously
produced, beautiful books. In the thirteenth-century context from

which we know these texts, whatever their origin, they are written
texts and their evocation of oral performance thus points towards
what I will call a *fiction of orality*. Lines such as these offer a written
representation of a minstrel singing the narrative. They conjure up
a fictional performance more than they represent an actual performance that the scribe who copied them ever witnessed. They
evince a nostalgia on the part of an essentially bookish culture in
the Middle Ages that is essentially similar to the nostalgia that leads
some modern critics to privilege the supposed oral origins of texts
like this.

References to writing are not uncommon in the *chansons de geste*,
even in the Oxford *Roland*, supposed by some to be the purest
monument to oral-formulaic style. Thus, when Ganelon goes as an
emissary to the Saracens he takes with him not just an orally transmitted message (which of course he fails to transmit accurately),
but also a letter (or more accurately a writ, since the document was
probably not closed, but rather open, with a seal at the bottom; see
Bennett):

> Marsilies fut tut desculurez d'ire,
> Freint le sëel, getét en ad la cire;
> Guardet al bref, vit la raisun ecrite.
>
> (*Roland*, 485-7)

(Marsilie was so angry his face changed colour, he breaks the
seal and throws down the wax; he looks at the letter and
reads what is written.)

Philip Bennett has argued that Marsilie's breaking of the seal is
an act of defiance, in that Charlemagne's image would have been
on it. It is not clear whether or not he reads the letter. However,
it is clear that the *Roland* portrays a world in which writing has a
part to play, which is familiar with the paraphernalia of documents, and in which some nobles are literate. More important
still than the representation of writing within the narrative frame
are references to the relation of the text we are reading to other
written texts:

> Dist l'arcevesques: 'Nostre hume sunt mult proz;
> Suz ciel n'ad rei plus en ait de meillors.
> Il est escrit en la Geste Francor
> Que bons vassals out nostre empereür'.
>
> (*Roland*, 1441-4)

(The archbishop says: 'Our men are very brave: no mortal king ever had any better. It is written in the *Legend of the French* that our emperor had fine vassals.')

> Ki puis veïst Rollant e Oliver
> De lur espees ferir e capleier!
> Li arcevesque i fiert de sun espiét.
> Cels qu'il unt mort, ben les poet hom preiser:
> Il est escrit es cartres e es brefs,
> Ço dit la Geste, plus de quatre milliers.
>
> (*Roland*, 1680-85)

(If only you could have seen Roland and Oliver striking out again and again with their swords! And the archbishop attacks with his lance too. The men that they have killed are indeed considered to be brave too. It is written in the charters and documents, so says the legend, that there were more than 4000 of them.)

If these references are to be taken seriously, they suggest written sources (or at least corroboration) for the content of the poem, while the use of the verb *dire* in line 1685 does not necessarily indicate an oral as opposed to a written text, since, as we have already seen, in a culture in which reading habitually meant reading aloud, verbs indicating aural interaction with a text are frequently used in written texts. Furthermore, although both these extracts are ambiguous, each could in fact be referring implicitly to the Oxford *Roland* itself as a written text: in the first case the *Geste Francor* could designate the text we are reading (the *Chanson de Roland* is a modern confection), and in the second there is no reason why the *Geste* could not be a written text, particularly in the context of the previous line.

Perhaps the strongest evidence for the bookishness of the *Roland* poet comes in the notoriously controversial last line, in which he may or may not name himself: 'Ci falt la geste que Turoldus declinet' (4002). Putting aside the identity of this mysterious Turoldus, the verb used here is intriguing. It has been attributed a variety of meanings: 'recite', 'compose', 'proclaim', 'transcribe', 'dies', 'grows weary' and so on. Its precise sense is unclear and there are no other examples of it being used in this way. It is nonetheless clear that used in relation to a linguistic performance (whether spoken or written), *declinet* is a Latinate word, associated as it is usually with the declension of Latin words. The use of such an apparently learned word as the last word of a poem surely sends a clear signal about the culture of the poet.

Selected Reading

La Chanson de Roland, ed. Ian Short (Paris, 1990)
Le Couronnement de Louis, ed. Ernest Langlois, second edition (Paris, 1968)

Joseph Bédier, *Les Légendes épiques* (Paris, 1914-21). Makes the case for the *chanson de geste* as a written genre.

Philip Bennett, 'Ganelon's false message: a critical false perspective?', in *Reading around the Epic. A Festschrift in Honour of Professor Wolfgang van Emden*, ed. Marianne Ailes, Philip Bennett and Karen Pratt (London, 1998), pp. 149-69. Careful study of the episode in which Ganelon takes a message to the Saracens.

Suzanne Fleischman, 'A linguistic perspective on the *laisses similaires*: orality and the pragmatics of narrative discourse', *Romance Philology*, 43 (1989-90), 70-89. Superlative analysis of some *laisses similaires*.

Jean Rychner, *La Chanson de Geste. Essai sur l'art épique des jongleurs* (Geneva, 1955). Influential essay on the formulaic style of the *chanson de geste* as evidence of orality.

Eugène Vinaver, 'La mort de Roland', *Cahiers de Civilisation Médiévale*, 7 (1964), 133-42. Excellent reading of the *laisses* analysed in this chapter.

See also the Selected Reading for the Introduction.

Writing and 'Oral' Style in Romance: The Case of Béroul's *Tristan*

Apart from the *chansons de geste*, the Old French material that is most commonly thought to derive from an oral tradition is the large quantity of romances and *lais* that draw on what is often called the *matière de Bretagne*, texts which ostensibly have Celtic sources. Tales of King Arthur and the knights of the Round Table, of the passionate but deadly love of Tristan and Yseult, and of assorted fairy lovers or supernatural encounters, are said to have made their way from Wales and Ireland to France in the first half of the twelfth century to inspire, in the first instance, the Latin writer Geoffrey of Monmouth, whose *Historia Regum Britanniae* was written between 1135 and 1138, then Wace, an Anglo-Norman poet working in the 1150s and 1160s. In due course, as we move through the 1170s, 80s and 90s, contributors to the Arthurian tradition in French include Chrétien de Troyes (perhaps the greatest of twelfth-century romancers and author of five surviving Arthurian romances: *Erec et Enide*, *Cligès*, *Yvain*, *Le Chevalier de la Charrete* and the unfinished *Conte du Graal*), Marie de France (one of the only women writers from the period whose work has survived), Béroul and Thomas (who wrote lengthy versions of the Tristan story that have only survived in fragmentary form), as well as numerous other writers of Arthurian verse romance, many of whom remain anonymous. The rapid translation of much of this material into German testifies to its wide dissemination, and early in the thirteenth century the two great Celtic narratives, the love stories of Lancelot and Guinevere and Tristan and Yseult, were transposed into vast prose cycles that were to remain popular for centuries, eventually to inspire writers like Malory.

Early romance

If early romance drawing on the *matière de Bretagne* did use oral sources, how 'oral' are these texts themselves? Wace, the earliest author of Arthurian narratives writing in French, had an overtly political project. Working in the domains of Henry II, his *Roman de Rou* and *Roman de Brut* sought to retell the history of Western Europe with a view to legitimising the claims of the upstart Plantagenet dynasty to the crown of England by allowing it to bask by analogy in the reflected glory of Arthur's legendary kingdom. But Wace's source for his Arthurian material was not oral: he used (albeit somewhat freely) the Latin text of his near contemporary Geoffrey of Monmouth and makes it clear, in any case, that his own texts are written texts, intended for reading aloud:

> Pur remembrer des ancesurs
> les feiz e les diz e les murs,
> les felunies des feluns
> e les barnages des baruns,
> deit l'um les livres e les gestes
> e les estoires lire a festes.
> Si escripture ne fust feite
> e puis par clers litte e retraite,
> mult fussent choses ubliees,
> ki de viez tens sunt trespassees.
>
> (*Rou*, 1-10)

(In order to remember the actions, words and customs of our ancestors, the felonious deeds of the felons and the worthy deeds of the worthy, one should read [aloud] books, heroic tales and stories at festivities. If writing had not been undertaken and then read and recopied by clerks, many things that happened in olden times would have been forgotten.)

Romance, here in its earliest incarnation, claims written sources. Romances are stories told from books. Working at the same time as Wace – and a little before the writers to whom modern readers devote most attention, Chrétien de Troyes, Marie de France, Thomas and Béroul – the authors of the so-called *romans antiques* (the *Roman d'Eneas*, the *Roman de Troie* and the *Roman de Thèbes*, free translations into French octosyllabic rhyming couplets of Latin texts) similarly make it clear that they have written sources and produce written texts. Consider, for example, Benoît de Sainte-Maure's opening of his *Troie* (c. 1165):

> E por ce me vuell travailler
> En une estoire conmencer,
> Que, de latin ou je la truis,
> Se j'ai le sens e se ge puis,
> Le voudrai si en romanz metre
> Que cil qui n'entendront la letre
> Se puissent deduire el romanz ...
> Ceste estoire n'est pas usee,
> N'en guaires lués nen est trovee;
> Ja retraite ne fust unquore,
> Mes Beneeiz de Sainte More
> La continue e fait e dit
> E o sa main les moz escrit.
>
> (33-9 and 129-34)

(And this is why I wish to work on a story which, if I am clever enough and am able to do so, I will translate from the Latin, as I found it, into the romance tongue [French] so that those who will not understand the [Latin] text can enjoy it in French ... this story is not worn out, nor is it found in many places: it has not been told before, but Benoît de Sainte-Maure continues and makes and says it and writes the words with his own hand.)

We might note here the juxtaposition of the verbs *dit* and *escrit* at the rhyme: writing incorporates rather than precludes orality.

Moreover, there is a real sense of excitement, in texts such as these, at the use of writing for the composition, dissemination and transmission of narrative material in French: through translation, Benoît continues a process of writing and rewriting begun in classical times. This is not to say that Arthurian stories had not previously circulated orally, or even that the classical material of the *romans antiques* did not circulate orally. But these first French romances seem conscious of the fact that theirs is a written medium.

What difference does the use of writing make to texts such as these, particularly when, as we have seen, they are intended for reading aloud and therefore for aural reception? The difference lies in the importance of the book and the consequent role of the author. Whereas oral traditions (obviously) identify the story-teller with the speaker, in a written tradition the author and the speaker/reader need not be one and the same person. A written tradition may therefore construct an author who is entirely separate from the narrator. Consider the way that Benoît de Sainte-Maure names himself in the third person in the last quotation: someone else can read aloud (and thereby narrate) Benoît's text, but he remains the author, or more accurately an author-figure within the text. As we will see, writing thereby enables, one might even say encourages, critical distance and irony as the author becomes a quasi-fictional, absent figure whose words are mediated through the book. Furthermore, ethnographic research suggests that whereas in an oral culture the traditional stories that are transmitted and retold by story-tellers belong to the culture as a whole so that the story-teller may become a mouth-piece for communal values, the distance between the author-figure and those listening to the story in a written culture necessarily changes this role. The author may become more powerful, a revealer of concealed, unknown truths rather than a purveyor of familiar ones. The reader (that is the person who reads the text aloud) mediates access to something otherwise inaccessible to the illiterate. Two points follow from this. First, you did not have to be literate to have access to written texts. Secondly, when a text is renarrating a familiar story, the material becomes less important than the manner of narration.

Or, to use a distinction suggested by Chrétien de Troyes, the *matiere* is subordinate to the *san* (sense or meaning, see below p. 94). How a text generates meaning (the hermeneutic process) becomes necessarily more complex when writing is used.

If we move on a few years from the *romans antiques*, to writers like Marie de France, Chrétien, Béroul and Thomas, critical consensus tells us that Béroul's *Tristan* shows signs of oral style, but that Thomas offers a much more bookish version of the story; it is similarly agreed that Marie and Chrétien composed written texts but drew on an oral, Celtic tradition as well as written texts, though recently Evelyn Birge Vitz has made a vigorous and polemical case for Chrétien being not a clerk, as is generally assumed, but a minstrel who worked in a purely oral medium (*Orality and Performance*, chapter 4). These perceptions derive from references to oral traditions and the apparently oral style of some of the texts themselves. In this chapter and the next, I wish to examine the value of references to oral sources and the seemingly oral style in some of this Celtic material with a view to considering the implications for story-telling and our own reading of these stories.

Béroul's *Tristan* and the voice in the text

Let us begin with Béroul whose style in his *Tristan* is said to be heavily marked by oral story-telling techniques. Here is a typical instance of his 'oral' style:

> Dedenz la chanbre n'out clartez,
> Cirge ne lanpë alumez.
> Tristan se fu sus piez levez.
> Dex! porqoi fist? Or escoutez!
> Les piez a joinz, emse, si saut,
> El lit le roi chaï de haut.
> Sa plaie escrive, forment saine;
> Le sanc qui' en ist les dras ensaigne.
> La plaie saigne; ne la sent,
> Qar trop a son delit entent.
> En plusors leus li sanc aüne.

Li nains defors est. A la lune
Bien vit josté erent ensemble
Li dui amant: de joie en trenble.
Et dist au roi: 'Se nes puez prendre
Ensemble, va, si me fai pendre.'

(725-40)

(There was no light in the chamber, neither candle nor lamp
burning. Tristan got to his feet. God, why did he do this? Now
listen! He's put his feet together, judges the distance and
leaps, falling into the king's bed from on high. His wound
opens and bleeds profusely. The blood that pours out stains
the sheets. His wound bleeds, but he doesn't feel it because
he is too intent on his pleasure. The blood gathers in several
places. The dwarf is outside; by the moonlight he sees the two
lovers in a close embrace: he trembles with joy. And he says
to the king: 'if you can't catch them together then go on,
string me up.')

Béroul's consummate skill as a story-teller is very much in evidence
here. The lovers' enemies, three wicked barons and the equally
despicable dwarf Frocin, aim to convince king Mark, not for the
first time, that his wife Yseult and his beloved nephew Tristan are
lovers. Having learnt that he is being sent temporarily away from
court on an errand, Tristan contrives to visit Yseult secretly in her
bed, as his enemies knew he would. Suspecting treachery, Tristan
notices flour spread on the floor around Yseult's bed so that his
footprints might leave clear evidence of their adultery. So he leaps
from his own bed into hers, leaping being one of Tristan's many
accomplishments: a little later in the Béroul fragment he makes a
death-defying leap from a chapel on a cliff in order to escape cap-
tivity. On this occasion, unfortunately, he forgets that he has a
superficial hunting wound on his leg, and he bleeds profusely in
the queen's bed. And so, despite there being no footprints in the
flour, he does leave evidence of his presence, which leads to them
both being taken into custody and to the aforementioned spectac-
ular second leap.

The scene gives a vivid sense of the conditions in which people
lived in twelfth-century courts: there is no private bed-chamber, since
doors and windows are open. The lovers are spied upon at every turn,
and if they seem to take pleasure in taking risks, the other characters,
like the dwarf, who trembles with joy when he sees them in bed
together, take a quasi-voyeuristic pleasure in watching them. The
involvement of the dwarf engrossed in watching the lovers is paralleled by the narrator's apparently enraptured involvement in the
scene, which in turn engenders our involvement (and pleasure) as
readers. As the narrative moves from the preterite (725-8, the
modern French past historic), to the perfect (729) and then into the
present (730-8), lending the action intense immediacy, the narrator
seems to explode with anxiety for the lovers before addressing the
audience directly and encouraging them to listen closely ('Dex!
porqoi fist? Or escoutez!'). The attention to detail, here as elsewhere
in Béroul, is meticulous: Tristan does not just leap, but he puts his
feet together and judges the distance before doing so.

On one level the 'orality' of Béroul's style in a passage like this
is beyond doubt. A live audience appears to be addressed by a first-
person, speaking narrator. Moreover, the text appears to have been
structured episodically in short chunks of narrative that are
thought to reflect individually performed episodes in an on-going
soap-opera style series. But does this mean then that Béroul's
Tristan is the work of an oral poet?

As with so many twelfth-century writers, Béroul portrays aristocratic society as familiar with writing. Thus after the lovers have
spent three years living in the forest, on the run but consummating
their love at will, they decide that they wish to return to court to
seek the advice of the hermit Ogrin. He suggests that they write
Mark a letter. This they do, but the main protagonists are not portrayed as literate themselves, since Tristan dictates his letter to
Ogrin (line 2430), while Mark has it read aloud to him:

> Li rois esvelle son barnage.
> Primes manda le chapelain,
> Le brief li tent qu'a en la main.
> Cil fraint la cire et lut le brief;

Li roi choisi el premier chief,
A qui Tristan mandoit saluz.
Les moz a tost toz conneüz,
Au roi a dit le mandement.
Li rois l'escoute bonement;
A grant mervelle s'en esjot,
Qar sa feme forment amot.

(2510-20)

(The king wakes his household. First he sent for the chaplain
and he gives him the letter he holds in his hand. The chaplain breaks the seal and read the letter; it is addressed to the
king to whom Tristan sent greetings. He has quickly deciphered all the words and tells the king what the message says.
The king listens attentively; he is wonderfully joyous since he
loved his wife very much.)

Mark then has the letter read to the whole court and it is repro-
duced exactly in the text (2556-618); he then replies to them by
letter, rather than sending a messenger. My point is that the society
portrayed in Béroul's *Tristan* is hardly an 'oral culture', reliant exclusively on the spoken word: on the contrary, it is a world familiar with
writing and in the habit of using writing to conduct its affairs.

How then does Béroul envisage his own story, as oral, or as
written? Famously, on two occasions he names himself while talking
about the status of his own text. On the first occasion, he takes issue
with an alternative version of the story, according to which Tristan
and his erstwhile mentor Governal killed Yvain, a leper to whom
Mark, in a fit of pique, had entrusted Yseult as sex-slave to punish her:

Li conteor dïent qu'Yvain
Firent nïer, qui sont vilain;
N'en sevent mie bien l'estoire,
Berox l'a mex en sen memoire:
Trop ert Tristan preuz et cortois
A occire gent de tes lois.

(1265-70)

(Some story-tellers, who are vile, say that they had Yvain
drowned; they don't know the story well. Béroul has remembered it better: Tristan was too worthy and courtly to kill such
people.)

Béroul is thought to be warning against the unreliability of other
minstrels' versions of the story. The use of the verb *dire* along with
the expression *aver mex en sen memoire* are taken as clear signs of the
orality of his own version. But *dire*, like *oïr* (to hear) is often used
in relation to *written* texts (see the *Roman de Troie*, 133 and Béroul's
Tristan, line 2517, both quoted above), while *memoire*, though it can
obviously evoke something learnt by heart, is also often associated
with writing:

> Mult soleient estre onuré
> e mult preisé e mult amé
> cil ki les gestes escriveient
> e ki les estoires treiteient;
> suvent aveient des baruns
> e des nobles dames beaus duns,
> pur mettre lur nuns en estoire,
> que tuz tens mais fust de eus memoire.
>
> (Wace, *Rou*, 143-50)

(The men who wrote the tales and told the stories used to be
greatly honoured, respected and loved; they often received
fine gifts from the barons and noble ladies so that their
names would be recorded in a story and so that they might
be remembered forever.)

As this and other examples of *memoire* in Old French suggest, to
write something down is to ensure it is remembered, and there are
several examples of *memoire* being used for a text (for example
'Ceus qui orront cest memoire'). Moreover, the Modern French
semantic distinction between *mémoire* as a masculine noun
(meaning a written text, usually a thesis) and *mémoire* as a feminine
noun (meaning 'memory') has not yet developed in Old French

and the word is indiscriminately masculine or feminine, so when Béroul writes 'Berox l'a mex en sen memoire', he might well mean that his written version of the story is more reliable.

On the second occasion he names himself in the surviving fragment, Béroul talks explicitly about writing:

> Ne, si conme l'estoire dit,
> La ou Berox le vit escrit,
> Nule gent tant ne s'entramerent
> Ne si griment nu conpererent.
>
> (1789-92)

(Never, as the story says, there where Béroul saw it written down, did anyone ever love each so much nor pay for it so dearly.)

In claiming a written source for his own text, Béroul inscribes his version of the story in a written rather than an oral tradition. But the fact that he distinguishes his version from those of his rivals, whether these be oral or written, and draws attention to the fact that there are competing versions is significant: we should note that his act of writing is also an act of reading (1790) and therefore of interpretation. Moreover, in both these instances of self-naming, Béroul refers to himself in the third-person, thereby making himself into a third-person author-figure, who is potentially at least separate from the narrator. The excitable, partisan and involved narrator whose anxiety for the lovers is palpable and who enjoins his listeners to pay attention, is a construct of the author who need not be the reader of this text for it to maintain its impact. To be sure, Béroul's *Tristan* would have required a skilled reader, capable of conveying the narrator's character as scripted by the author. But the oral/aural effectiveness of the narrative rests first and foremost on the words recorded on the page. The voice in this text is not free to say what it likes.

In a print culture, texts are usually (though by no means always) relatively stable. In a manuscript culture, every author, indeed every scribe, can change a story as he transmits it. But this instability differs radically from the inherent instability of oral texts: whereas (at least before the invention of modern recording technology) every performance of an orally transmitted narrative disappears as it unfolds, the written text in a manuscript survives. Whereas a purely oral narrative always refers back to its lost beginning, existing in a continuous present before expiring, a written narrative (whether read silently or aloud) anticipates its textual future by anticipating future readers. A written text anticipates its own survival and relative fixity. My contention is that twelfth-century writers were quite conscious of the difference between written and oral texts and that they exploited the differences to great effect.

Selected Reading

Benoît de Sainte-Maure: *Le Roman de Troie*, ed. Emmanuèle Baumgartner and Françoise Vielliard (Paris, 1998)

Béroul: *Roman de Tristan*, in *Tristan et Iseut: les poèmes français et la saga norroise*, ed. and trans. Daniel Lacroix and Philippe Walters (Paris, 1989)

Wace: *Le Roman de Rou*, ed. Anthony J. Holden, 3 vols. (Paris, 1970-73)

Emmanuèle Baumgartner, *Tristan et Iseult: essai de lecture plurielle* (Paris, 1987). Good general introduction to the Old French Tristan poems.

Alberto Varvaro, *Béroul's Romance of Tristan* (Manchester, 1972). Still useful close reading of the text.

Vitz, *Orality and Performance*, see Selected Reading for the Introduction

3

Fictions of Orality in Marie de France's *Lais*

One writer who alludes persistently to oral traditions is Marie de France. Marie, like most French writers of the period, is a mysterious figure about whom we know virtually nothing for certain, but the uncertainties that surround the authorship of the texts that have been attributed to her are particularly intriguing. She seems to have been a French woman living in England and writing therefore for the ruling Norman classes. The *Lais* are dedicated to a *noble reis* (*Prologue*, 43), generally thought to be Henry II, and Marie's writing career must therefore predate his death in 1189. She is best known for her *Lais*, but two other surviving works are commonly (though not securely) attributed to her: the *Fables* (an extensive collection of translations of *Aesops' Fables*) and the *Espurgatoire Saint Patrice* (a saint's life). The attribution of these works to the same writer rests largely on the use of the name Marie alongside an insistence on posterity:

> Oëz, seignur, que dit Marie,
> ki en sun tens pas ne s'oblie.
>
> (*Guigemar*, 3-4)

(Listen, my lords, to what Marie, who is not to be forgotten in her life-time, says.)

> Jo, Marie, ai mis en memoire,
> le livre de l'Espurgatoire,
> en romanz, qu'il seit entendables
> a laie gent e covenables.
>
> (*Espurgatoire*, quoted in *Lais*, p. 7)

(I, Marie, have rescued from oblivion the book of the *Espurgatoire*, in French, so that it might be understood by and suitable for lay people.)

> Al finement de cest escrit
> qu'en romanz ai treité et dit
> me numerai pur remembrance:
> Marie ai nun, si sui de France.
> (epilogue to the *Fables*, quoted in *Lais*, pp. 7-8)

(At the end of this text which I have translated and said in French, I will name myself so as not to be forgotten: my name is Marie and I am from France.)

The name 'Marie' is scarcely unusual and so to identify oneself as 'Marie from France' (the name Marie de France is in fact a post-medieval confection based on these lines from the *Fables*) is not unlike identifying oneself as John from England. In the *Espurgatoire*, it is the text that 'Marie' ostensibly wishes to save from oblivion, but in the other two texts it is the author herself who wishes to be remembered. What lies behind this oddly nebulous insistence on personal posterity?

Perhaps an answer is to be found in the *Lais*, since they treat authorship itself and remembrance as a theme. The *Lais* of Marie de France, as we read them in modern editions, are an anthology of twelve short narratives with a Celtic flavour preceded by a general prologue. However, the collection in this form is found in just one manuscript (known as Harley 978), now kept in the British Library: virtually all the *Lais* in the Harley collection survive in other collections of *lais* in which they are not attributed to Marie or even necessarily associated with each other. Although modern scholars, with a few notable exceptions such as Baum and Masters, have rarely questioned the authenticity of the Harley compilation, they are simply one collection of *Lais* among others, and the attribution of the twelve Harley *lais* to a figure called Marie (de France) who assembled them into a carefully structured sequence of short stories is less than secure. The author has a fragile hold on these texts, which is intriguing, given that the fragile hold an author of medieval texts has over her work is a recurring preoccupation of Marie's *Lais*. For the moment I will suspend consideration of the authorship of the Harley *Lais*, but I will return to this question after an examination of orality, writing and story-telling in these wonderfully evocative and clever stories.

Considerably shorter and less complex than the romances of figures like Béroul, Thomas and Chrétien de Troyes, *lais* share with romance the use of the octosyllabic rhyming couplet and like romances often have love as their main theme. Supernatural events are commonplace in *lais*: in Marie's *Lais*, to give but a few examples, we find an androgynous talking doe who curses the hero and a magic ship that guides lovers towards each other (*Guigemar*), a werewolf (*Bisclavret*), a fairy lover (*Lanval*), a magic potion (*Les Dous Amanz*), a knight prone to shape-shifting either to become a bird or to take the form of his beloved (*Yonec*), a magic herb that will revive the dead (*Eliduc*).

It is common in all *lais*, not just those attributed to Marie, to evoke Breton oral sources going back to the time of the events narrated, with the Celtic associations explaining the magic. *Lais* are therefore implicitly represented as sung (or at least accompanied by an instrument), Breton and relayed from generation to generation:

> Le lai escoutent d'Aiëlis
> que uns Irois doucement note,
> mout le sonnë en sa route.
> Apriés celi, d'autre commenche,
> nus d'iaus n'i noise ne n'i tenche;
> le lai lor sone d'Orpheÿ.
>
> (*Lai de l'Aubépine*, 178-83)

(They listen to the *Lai d'Aiëlis*, which an Irishman sweetly sings, strumming along on his *rote* [a stringed instrument]. After that another begins, and not one of them objects or remonstrates; he sings them the *Lai d'Orpheÿ*.)

Doon, cest lai sevent plusor:
n'i a gueres bon harpëor
ne sache les notes harper;
nes ie vos voil dire e conter
l'aventure dont li Breton
apelerent cest lai Doon.

(*Lai de Doon*, 1-6)

(Quite a few people know this *lai* about *Doon*: there are hardly any good harpists who do not know how to play the tune; and I wish to tell you and relate the adventure which led the Bretons to call this *lai Doon*.)

Marie, like the narrators of these anonymous *lais*, claims oral origins for her tales and makes references to their being sung:

Des lais pensai qu'oïz aveie.
Ne dutai pas, bien le saveie,
que pur remembrance les firent
des aventures qu'il oïrent
cil ki primes les comencierent
e ki avant les enveierent.
Plusurs en ai oïz conter,
nes vueil laissier ne oblïer.
Rime en ai e fait ditié,
soventes feiz en ai veillié.

(*Prologue*, 33-42)

(I thought about the *lais* I had heard. I did not doubt, indeed I was sure of this, that the people who first started telling and disseminating them composed them because they wished the adventures they heard to be remembered. I have heard quite a few related and I do not wish to abandon or forget them. I have rhymed and structured them, often working through the night.)

De cest cunte qu'oï avez
fu Guigemar li lais trovez,

> que hum fait en harpe e en rote;
> bone en est a oïr la note.
>
>   (*Guigemar*, 883-6)

(The *lai Guigemar*, which is accompanied by a harp and *rote*, was composed about this story that you have heard; the tune is pleasant to hear.)

> Mult unt esté noble barun
> cil de Bretaigne, li Bretun.
> Jadis suleient par pruësce,
> par curteisie e par noblesce
> des aventures que oeient,
> ki a plusurs genz aveneient,
> faire les lais pur remembrance,
> qu'um nes meïst en ubliance.
> Un en firent, ceo oi cunter,
> ki ne fet mie a ubliër,
> d'Equitan ki mult fu curteis.
>
>   (*Equitan*, 1-11)

(The men of Brittany, the Bretons, were very noble barons. In olden times, because of their worth, their courtesy and nobility, they used to compose *lais* about the adventures they heard that happened to many people so that they might be remembered and not forgotten. They composed one that I heard which is unforgettable, about Equitan who was so very courtly.)

But the persistent references to the origins of the tales among generations of Breton story-tellers (see also *Equitan*, 317-18, *Le Fraisne*, 533-6, *Les Dous Amanz*, 1-6 and 253-4, *Yonec*, 559-62, *L'Aüstic*, 1-6 and 159-60, *Chaitivel*, 1-2 and 231-40, *Eliduc*, 1181-4) do not indicate that Marie's *Lais* in themselves are purely oral stories. They have an interesting counterpoint in a series of references not only to *written* sources, but also to the written status of Marie's own compositions:

Les contes que jo sai verais,
dunt li Breton unt fait les lais,
vos conterai assez briefment.
El chief de cest comencement
sulunc la letre e l'escriture
vos mosterrai une aventure,
ki en Bretaigne la menur
avint al tens anciënur.

(*Guigemar*, 19-26)

(I will briefly tell you the tales that I know to be true about which the Bretons composed *lais*. As this work opens, according to what is recorded in writing, I will relate for you an adventure from olden times that came about in Brittany.)

De lur amur e de lur bien
firent un lai li ancïen;
e jeo ki l'ai mis en escrit
el recunter mult me delit.

(*Milun*, 531-4)

(The people from olden times composed a *lai* about their love and happiness; and I, who transposed it to writing, take great pleasure in relating it.)

Asez me plest e bien le vueil
del lai qu'um nume Chievrefueil
que la verité vus en cunt
coment fu fez, de quei e dunt.
Plusur le m'unt cunté e dit
e jeo l'ai trové en escrit
de Tristram e de la reïne.

(*Chievrefueil*, 1-7)

(It pleases me and gives me pleasure to tell you the truth about the *lai* that is known as *Chievrefueil*, how it was composed, about what and why. Quite a few people have told and

related it to me and I found it written down, about Tristan
and the queen.)

It would seem that the more frequent references to singing, orality
and oral traditions are belied by the fact that Marie is working in a
written tradition and clearly proud of her own written compositions. Moreover, as we will see, in the *Prologue* to the *Lais* she
displays her knowledge of Latin, as if to draw attention to her literacy and learning. Marie is a *writer*, so why does she seek
sometimes *to give the impression* that her stories are oral compositions possibly intended to be sung? Why does she stress her debt to
an oral tradition? And should we take her claims to have oral
sources at face value?

   The world that Marie portrays in her *Lais* is one in which writing
plays an important role in the lives of the glamorous aristocrats
who are her heroes and heroines. In *Milun*, for example, letters
play a crucial role. Thus at the beginning, the nameless heroine
asks her lover Milun to help her conceal their illegitimate child
from her father:

> 'Quant li enfes,' fait ele, 'iert nez,
> a ma serur l'en porterez,
> ki en Norhumbre est mariëe,
> riche dame, pruz e senee,
> si li manderez par escrit
> e par paroles e par dit
> que c'est li enfes sa serur,
> si'n a sufert meinte dolur.
> Or guart que il seit bien nurriz,
> quels que ço seit, u fille u fiz.
> Vostre anel al col li pendrai
> e un brief li enveierai;
> escriz i iert li nuns sun pere
> e l'aventure de sa mere.
> Quant il sera granz e creüz
> e en tel eage venuz
> que il sace raisun entendre,

le brief e l'anel li deit rendre,
si li cumant tant a guarder
que sun pere puisse trover.'

(*Milun*, 67-86)

('When the child is born,' she says, 'take him to my married
sister in Northumberland, a rich, worthy and wise lady, and
convey to her in writing and through your speech and words
that this is her sister's child and that she has suffered great
pain because of it. She should take care to bring it up well,
whether it is a girl or a boy. I will hang your ring around its
neck and send a letter for him; his father's name will be in it
and his mother's story. When he is older and grown and
reached the age where he can understand, she should give
him the ring and the letter and tell him to keep them so that
he might find his father.')

In due course the child's aunt gives him the ring and the letter,
from which he learns his father's name. But before we are told how
he finds his father, we hear at some length of the lovers' continued
communication by letter over a period of twenty years while the
unhappy heroine is married to another: Milun has a tame swan
that they use to carry letters. As Sarah Spence argues, Marie
exploits throughout this episode a bookish pun on the homo-
phones *cigne* ('swan') and *signe* ('sign'), which may imply a literate
audience, trained to be alert to puns of this kind. It is clear that the
couple read and write the letters themselves. The ability to read
and write does not seem worthy of remark here, and the lovers use
writing as a surrogate for face-to-face contact. Fittingly, at the end
of *Milun*, as father and son set out to find a way of uniting the
family, they receive another letter announcing the convenient
death of the inconvenient husband and, in a rather Freudian fan-
tasy, the son gives his mother to his father (527-8).

The story of *Milun* relies on writing and these are not the only
lovers in the *Lais* for whom writing is important. In *Chievrefueil*, to
which I will return presently, Tristan writes a message for his lover
on a stick and she, like the heroine of *Milun*, seems to have no

trouble reading. Marie's *Lais* are written texts about a world in which writing is taken for granted, and we might therefore infer from this that they address an audience similarly familiar with writing. As with Béroul's *Tristan*, the orality of Marie's *Lais* is feigned and fictional. However, the repeated insistence on oral sources suggests that the oral tradition to which Marie appeals has a value both to her and to her public, that it is being deployed for a specific purpose. It would appear that this value is twofold.

First, the value ascribed to an antecedent oral tradition in the twelfth century was similar to the value ascribed to oral traditions today by scholars of orality: whereas writing is thought to be arch, indirect, potentially devious and calculating, the oral tradition claims authenticity, immediacy and sincerity. Hence Marie's repeated claims to truth (see *Guigemar*, 19 and *Bisclavret*, 316) which are supported by the stories' ostensible provenance from eye witnesses, contemporaries, or on two occasions the protagonists themselves (*Chaitivel* and *Chievrefueil*). The oral tradition that Marie evokes suggests a nostalgia for the immediacy and unproblematic authenticity of a world before writing, a world prone to magic solutions to insoluble problems. However, since she portrays this world from the perspective of a written culture, Marie's gesture towards orality is disingenuous: the oral tradition exists within the fictional frame of writing and is dependent on it. Tellingly, if analogues in Celtic folklore have been found for some of Marie's *Lais*, the 'oral sources' for others seem to have left no other traces. It is quite possible that Marie made some of her *aventures* up, rather than hearing them from Breton bards. In any case, where the stories really came from is less important than the appeal to orality itself, which is a rhetorical ploy to make us read the narrative in a certain way. Marie's *Lais* are often praised for their simplicity, for their direct and uncomplicated appeal to the emotions and these qualities are sometimes ascribed to her being a woman. But if, as I hope I have shown, the qualities for which she is admired (which depend to a large extent on the feigned orality of her written texts), are highly contrived, then they are the result of a writer's skill and intelligence as much as a woman's intuition.

I would suggest, however, that the second value of orality in

Marie's *Lais* is intimately bound up with her gender and, in my
view, offers the most compelling grounds for seeing the Harley
Lais as the result of a single authorial project and the work of a
woman. Orality, in Marie's *Lais*, is used to figure the fragile hold
authors have on their texts because of the vagaries of transmission
in a manuscript culture, but the problems of authorship are portrayed as particularly acute for women. Let us now take a closer
look at the question of authorship in the *Lais*, which is intimately
entwined with the question of what the text itself is.

In the *Prologue* to the *Lais*, the author famously displays her
Latinate learning and toys with writing more *romans antiques*
before, as we have seen, rejecting this cultural tradition in favour
of *lais* (33-42, quoted above) and then offering her own personal
anthology to the *nobles reis* (43-56):

> Custume fu as anciëns,
> ceo testimoine Preciëns,
> es livres que jadis faiseient
> assez oscurement diseient
> pur cels ki a venir esteient
> e ki aprendre les deveient,
> que peüssent gloser la letre
> e de lur sen le surplus metre ...
> Pur ceo començai a penser
> d'alkune bone estoire faire
> e de Latin en Romanz traire;
> mais ne me fust guaires de pris:
> itant s'en sont altre entremis.
>
> (9-16 and 28-32)

(As Priscian tells us, it was the custom of the ancients in the
books they composed in those days to speak obscurely to
those who were to come later and study them, so that these
people might gloss their texts and add their own layer of
wisdom ... For this reason I began to think about composing
some good story or other, translated from Latin into French;
but I decided this was of no value: others have done this.)

The *Prologue* therefore seems explicitly to reject a Latinate – implicitly written – tradition in favour of an oral one that hails from the exotic world of the Celtic fringes, then as now associated with fairies, giants and supernatural happenings. Marie's decision to compose *lais* has been interpreted as a gendered choice: rejecting a written culture dominated by men in favour of an oral culture to which women have free access, Marie uses the genre of the Breton *lai* in order to make a specifically and authentically feminine voice heard (see Rosenn). But this does not mean that there is anything *inherently* feminine about orality or about the Breton *lai*: the point is that the *Lais* represent a textual space that is marked as different from the learned sphere of the Latinate *romans antiques*, which Marie associates by implication in her *Prologue* with male writers. Because Marie is a woman writer, this claim to occupy a different space becomes gendered, which is no doubt a deliberate ploy on her part. However, since the texts that she produces are written texts, we are confronted once again not with oral texts, but with written representations of oral texts. Moreover, Marie's subtle account of the textuality of the *lais* we are about to read in the *Prologue* warrants careful scrutiny for she is careful to imply that if she wanted to write texts like everyone else (as it were like the boys translating from Latin), she is perfectly capable of doing so. She thereby stakes her own claim to Latinity while saying she is not interested in it. But if her texts are written texts, how different are they? And if the stories she is offering the noble king are popular stories, what exactly is the nature of the labour which makes her so proud (41-2)?

Since Marie claims repeatedly not to have made the stories up herself, but to have heard them from others, claiming furthermore that many of them are true, her gift is less the stories themselves than the way that she tells them. In a sense this makes her *Lais* remarkably similar to the tales derived from Latin that ostensibly she is rejecting, in that 'glossing the text' and 'adding her own layer of wisdom' is precisely what she is doing (or more accurately, if she did make some of the stories up, claiming to be doing). Her formulation about the customs of the ancients is telling, for it suggests that the ancients wrote in such a way as to invite and anticipate subsequent glossing, interpretation and rewriting ('lur sen le surplus metre'). A text is not represented here as inviolably fixed and immutable, but on the contrary as mobile, susceptible to transformation as it is interpreted. A text, in other words, does not belong inviolably to its author, but can be appropriated and retold by others as they add their own layer of wisdom. This is precisely what seems to happen with *lais*, but a number of Marie's *Lais* suggest that there are different stakes for men and women in the transmission of textual material.

This may be inferred, for example, from Marie's most exquisite and delicate *lai*: *L'Aüstic*. In this brief tale a woman's apparently chaste love is symbolised by the song of the nightingale she listens to at the same time as her lover, who is a neighbour, as they sit in their separate dwellings. Her irascible husband kills the nightingale when she claims that it is the reason she is unable to sleep, spending hours at the window where her lover can see her. In a fit of rage the husband throws the dead bird at his wife, staining her dress with blood. In the face of this violent symbolic death of her love, the lady laments the demise of her nocturnal musical concourse with her *ami* and is concerned lest he think she no longer love him:

> 'Une chose sai jeo de veir,
> il quidera que jeo me feigne.
> De ceo m'estuet que cunseil preigne:
> l'aüstic or li trametrai,
> l'aventure li manderai!'
> En une piece de samit,
> a or brusdé e tut escrit,
> a l'oiselet envolupé.
> Un suen vaslet a apelé.
> Sun message li a chargié,
> a sun ami l'a enveié.
> Cil est al chevalier venuz.
> De sa dame li dist saluz,
> tut sun mesage li cunta
> e l'aüstic li presenta.

Quant tut li a dit e mustré
e il l'aveit bien esculté,
de l'aventure esteit dolenz;
mes ne fu pas vileins ne lenz.
Un vaisselet a fet forgier.
Unkes n'i ot fer ne acier:
tuz fu d'or fin od bones pieres,
mult preciüses e mult chieres;
covercle i ot tresbien asis.
L'aüstic aveit dedenz mis;
puis fist la chasse enseeler,
tuz jurs l'a faite od lui porter.
Cele aventure fu cuntee,
ne pot estre lunges celee.
Un lai en firent li Bretun
e l'Aüstic l'apelë hum.

(130-60)

('I know one thing for certain, that he will think that I am weary of his love. I have to do something. I will send him the nightingale and the story of what has happened!' She has embroidered with gold writing a piece of silk cloth in which she has wrapped the little bird. She has called a servant. She has given him her message and sent him to her lover. He has come to the knight. He greeted him on behalf of his lady, told him the whole message and gave him the nightingale. When he had said and explained everything to him and when the knight had listened carefully, he was much saddened by the story; but he was neither unworthy nor slow on the uptake. He had a casket forged. There was no iron or steel in it: rather it was made of pure gold with precious and rare stones; it had a well-fitting cover. When he had placed the nightingale in it, he had the casket sealed and had it carried everywhere he went. The story was told near and far, since it could not be kept a secret for long. The Bretons composed a *lai* about it which is called *L'Aüstic*.)

On one level, the knight would seem to behave in a courtly and worthy manner here as the narrator claims (148): he treats the pitiful symbol of his lost love with great honour as a holy relic. Of course, this may be what the lady instructs him to do in her message or in the writing on the cloth, but Marie is silent as to the content of both, deliberately leaving what the lady wants open to interpretation. Does the knight in fact do as she wanted? Why did she decide to write her story down and send it to him? The fact that she sends him a message implies that for her their love is not over (130-34) and we might infer therefore that in some respects his behaviour is precisely the opposite of what she intended. He treats their love as a thing of the past, to be commemorated, dead along with the bird; she treats their love as something to be kept alive despite the bird's demise.

The lady's text is taken away from her forever, placed in a casket that will prevent others from reading it: her writing is tightly sealed off from the world, its meaning dictated by the knight's interpretation (or mis-interpretation?). Critics have highlighted Marie's extraordinarily subtle, layered representation of textuality here (see notably Freeman and Griffin). The bird itself is a kind of text, since it symbolises something for the lovers; it is wrapped in the lady's text (the embroidered cloth), which is then contained in the knight's casket, a form of interpretation. But fortunately the chain of transmission does not stop there: the Bretons compose a *lai* about the story, which one day Marie (allegedly) hears in order to compose *L'Aüstic*, the text we read. This is therefore a text about a text and the text is figured rather like a Russian doll: you remove one layer to reveal another. The process that makes this possible, the chain of textual transmission, is very much to the fore in this short text, which is a narrative of textual loss as much as the loss of love. What constitutes the final layer, the core? Perhaps the dead nightingale, which figures the loss of love song and the loss of the desire which is associated with its song (see Huot). But significantly the lady's attempt to keep her love alive is transformed into an act of commemoration that ultimately Marie foregrounds to show the tenuous hold this woman has on her own story. Telling the story of the story thereby becomes a blow for female authorship in that it narrates a woman's loss of control of her own text.

L'Aüstic is not the only one of Marie's *Lais* in which female authorship is treated as a central theme. In *Chaitivel* four knights fall in love with the same worthy lady. Critics sometimes blame the heroine of *Chaitivel* for the story's tragic outcome, but I think it is worth remembering that the narrator insists upon her good judgement (49) and underlines the knights' responsibility for what happens (64). The lady in fact in some ways behaves in an exemplary courtly manner in that she treats all her suitors equally. All four take part in a tournament wearing a token from her: unfortunately they are so foolhardy that three are killed and the fourth wounded in such a way as to reduce his appeal as the male lead in a love story (122-3 : 'e li quarz nafrez e malmis / par mi la quisse e enz el corz', 'and the fourth wounded and incapacitated in the region of his thighs and on his body'). The lady is understandably stricken with grief and she visits her surviving suitor, while lamenting the loss of the others (177-80). She tells him of her decision to compose a *lai* about what has happened (193-204), which she intends to call *Les Quatre Doels* (*The Four Sorrows*) since 'vueil que mis doels seit remembrez' (202: I wish that my pain be commemorated'). But her erstwhile suitor is not happy with this:

> 'Dame, faites le lai novel,
> si l'apelez Le Chaitivel!
> E jeo vus vueil mustrer raisun
> que il deit issi aveir nun.
> Li altre sunt pieç' a finé
> e trestut le siecle unt usé
> en la grant peine qu'il sufreient
> de l'amur qu'il vers vus aveient.
> Mes jo ki sui eschapez vis,
> tuz esguarez e tuz chaitis,
> ceo qu'el siecle puis plus amer
> vei sovent venir e aler,
> parler od mei matin e seir,
> si n'en puis nule joie aveir

ne de baisier ne d'acoler
ne d'altre bien fors de parler.
Tels cent mals me faites sufrir,
mielz me valdreit la mort tenir.
Pur c'iert li lais de mei nomez:
"Le Chaitivel" iert apelez.
Ki "Quatre Doels" le numera,
sun propre nun li changera.'
'Par fei', fet ele, 'ceo m'est bel.
Or l'apelum "Le Chaitivel".'

Issi fu li lais comenciez
e puis parfaiz e anunciez.
Icil kil porterent avant,
'Quatre Doels' l'apelent alquant.
Chascuns des nuns bien i afiert,
kar la matire le requiert;
Le Chaitivel a nun en us.
Ici finist, il n'i a plus:
plus n'en oï ne plus n'en sai
ne plus ne vus en cunterai.

(207-40)

('My lady, by all means compose the new *lai*, but call it *Chaitivel* [the unfortunate one]! And I want to tell you why it should be called this. The others are recently dead and they used up in their lifetimes all their great sorrow in the love they bore you. But I, who escaped with my life, miserably and wretched, can see the thing I most love in the world coming and going all the time, speaking to me morning and night, but I can have no joy of her and I cannot kiss or embrace her or benefit from her presence in any way other than in talking. Thus you make me suffer a hundred times over and I would rather be dead. This is why the *lai* should be named after me: it should be called *Chaitivel*. Whoever calls it *The Four Sorrows* is changing its rightful name.' 'Very well,' she says, 'I agree. Let's call it *Chaitivel*.'

3. *Fictions of Orality in Marie de France's* Lais

Thus was the *lai* begun and then improved and disseminated. Some of those who told it call it *Four Sorrows*. Both names are appropriate, for the subject matter permits it. It is usually called *Chaitivel*. It finishes here and there is no more: I never heard nor do I know any more, nor will I tell you any more.)

The knight's response here is not only profoundly self-centred and self-serving, it represents an appropriation and misunderstanding of the lady's putative *lai* (see Sturges). Whereas she wishes to commemorate her feelings with the title of the *lai* she intends to compose, representing what *she* feels about her former suitors, he assumes the 'four sorrows' refer to the feelings of the four men and then puts forward an argument to prove that he has more reason to feel sorry for himself than the other three that have died, hence his suggested title, *Chaitivel*. He is oblivious to her sorrow and to her meaning. Despite the fact that the lady politely agrees to the title he suggests, the *lai* concludes with the narrator telling us that both titles are used, even if one is more frequent. It would seem, therefore, that the dispute over the title of this *lai* is not resolved. The text is open to interpretation and the alternative titles flag diverging readings according to which either the lady or the knight should be pitied and seen as the subject of the text, but not both (as the knight makes clear). So whose *lai* is this and which *lai* are we talking about? The text seems to suggest that the *lai* the lady composed is the basis of the *lai* that we are reading (both are known as either *Les Quatre Doels* or *Chaitivel*), but the *lai* we are reading has clearly been retold and reworked by many story-tellers other than the lady. It has also been given a title that is different from the one she originally intended, even if she did politely agree to this transformation.

Chaitivel, like *L'Aüstic*, stages a fiction of its own transmission which foregrounds the expropriation of a woman's text by a man, but, even more explicitly than *L'Aüstic*, *Chaitivel* invites its audience to ponder the implications of this. Of course it is possible that we are invited to believe that the lady is responsible for the fate of her suitors, but if this is the case we are nowhere told this explicitly. It is far more striking that we are left with two ways of taking hold of this clever and provocative little text.

Part of the provocation to interpret here stems from the seemingly deliberate confusion that is generated about what the text is. Conflicting signals about the oral or written nature of the *lais* combine with fictions of their origin, composition and transmission to leave the reader baffled in any given instance as to whether any given usage of the term *lai* designates (a) a Breton song composed shortly after the 'adventure' it relates sometimes by one of the protagonists, (b) a derivative of this song, (c) a poem in French allegedly derived from one of these songs. This uncertainty about the text is enhanced by Marie's dramatisation of the susceptibility of a woman's text to appropriation and transformation.

Of course *all* medieval texts are susceptible to appropriation and transformation, not just texts written by women. A prime illustration of this is Marie's delightful and moving *Chievrefueil.* Again this is a text which in part at least is about its own genesis. Exiled from court, the legendary lover Tristan longs to contrive a meeting with Yseult. As already noted, he writes a message for her on a stick which he leaves across her path and which, somewhat miraculously, she sees: it takes a discerning reader of signs to pick out a stick left in a wood as a signal! The message encourages her to slip away from her retinue for a brief encounter, in commemoration of which she tells Tristan to compose a *lai*, which turns out to be what we have just heard:

> Pur la joie qu'il ot eüe
> de s'amie q'il ot veüe
> e pur ceo qu'il aveit escrit,
> si cum la reïne l'ot dit,
> pur les paroles remembrer,
> Tristram ki bien saveit harper,
> en aveit fet un nuvel lai.
> Asez briefment le numerai:
> 'Gotelef' l'apelent Engleis,
> 'Chievrefueil' le nument Franceis.

> Dit vus en ai la verité,
> del lai que j'ai ici cunté.

>   (107-118)

(Because of the joy that he had had with his lover whom he had seen, and because of what he had written, just as the queen had told him to, in order to commemorate their words, Tristan, who played the harp well, composed a new *lai* about it. I will tell you briefly what it is called: the English call it 'Honeysuckle', the French call it *Chievrefueil.* I have told you the truth about the *lai* that I have narrated here.)

This is clearly a fictional account of the *lai*'s origin. Again a series of questions about authorship and textuality arise. Who is the 'author' of this text: Tristan, the queen who commanded him to compose it and who therefore is in some ways its point of origin, the English or the French who transmit the poem, or Marie who tells it to us? Again we are offered an apparently layered text of unclear origin.

Appropriately enough, at the heart of this *lai* there is further textual uncertainty. What exactly is the message that Tristan writes on the stick?

> Ceo fu la sume de l'escrit
> qu'il li aveit mandé e dit,
> que lunges ot ilec esté
> e atendu e surjurné
> pur espiër e pur saveir
> coment il la peüst veeir
> kar ne poeit vivre senz li.
> D'els dous fu il tut altresi
> cume del chievrefueil esteit
> ki a la coldre se perneit;
> quant il s'i est laciez e pris
> e tut entur le fust s'est mis,
> ensemble poeent bien durer;
> mes ki puis les vuelt desevrer,

la coldre muert hastivement
e li chievrefueilz ensement.
'Bele amie, si est de nus:
ne vus senz mei ne jeo senz vus!'

(61-78)

(This was what the writing he sent to her said, that he had
been there a long time waiting and tarrying to spy and see
how he could see her, for he could not live without her. The
two of them were just like the honeysuckle that clings to the
hazel; once it is wrapped around it fast and grown about its
trunk, they can only survive together; but if they are then sep-
arated the hazel dies at once and the honeysuckle too. 'Fair
lover, thus it is with us two: you cannot live without me, nor I
without you.')

This exquisite and memorable image encapsulates the intensity of
Tristan and Yseult's fatal love, deflecting attention from a problem
that has exercised scholars for well over a hundred years now. Did
Tristan really write all this on a stick? Is the text here rather a para-
phrase? Or are we rather to understand that only the last two lines
were actually written on the stick, with the rest simply the meaning
inferred by Yseult? The precise meaning of *la sume de l'escrit* is dis-
puted and unclear. The important point, it seems to me, is that
Chievrefueil offers a sophisticated meditation on writing and textuality: what we are reading may not be what was written, what we
understand may not be what was meant, and we don't really know
who wrote it. A text is always more than the sum of its parts (the
words on the page): what Tristan writes on the stick is considerably
less important than how Yseult interprets what he writes on the
stick.

    The *Lais* are not straightforward, traditional and 'oral' folktales.
They are highly self-conscious, fictionalising as they do their own
origins and transmission to create a textual space that depends on
an awareness of the power and value of storytelling as an act of
commemoration. They evoke oral origins not out of naivety, but in
order to enhance their own authenticity and create an aura of

innocent 'truth'. They use and celebrate writing while persuasively claiming the innocence of oral story-telling. Moreover, the repeated representation of the fragile hold story-tellers have on their narratives suggests a deliberate project in the *Lais* to push this issue to the fore, particularly in relation to women. This may suggest this compilation of *lais* had a single author and that this author was a woman. The *Lais* commemorate the Marie we are enjoined to listen to at the beginning of *Guigemar* even more effectively than if she had composed a *lai* about herself, for we have indeed not forgotten her, and this despite the fact that we know virtually nothing about her. But she owes this *remembrance* to writing: oral story-telling commemorates the story; writing can commemorate the writer as well as the story and Marie knew this.

Selected Reading

Lais féeriques du XIIe et XIIIe siècles, ed. Alexandre Micha (Paris, 1992)

Marie de France: *Lais,* ed. Karl Warnke and trans. Laurence Harf-Lancner (Paris, 1990)

Richard Baum, *Recherches sur les oeuvres attribuées à Marie de France* (Heidelberg, 1968). Examines manuscript evidence for an author called 'Marie de France'.

Matilda Bruckner, *Shaping Romance: Interpretation, Truth and Closure in Twelfth-Century French Fictions* (Philadelphia, 1993). Good chapter on Marie, with useful analysis of authorship and textuality in the *Lais*.

Michelle Freeman, 'Marie de France's poetics of silence: the implications for a feminine *translatio*', *PMLA,* 99 (1984), 860-83. Influential early feminist reading.

Miranda Griffin, 'Gender and authority in the medieval French lai', *Forum for Modern Language Studies,* 35 (1999), 42-56. Brilliant and witty feminist reading.

Sylvia Huot, 'Troubadour lyric and Old French narrative', in *The Troubadours: an Introduction,* ed. Simon Gaunt and Sarah Kay (Cambridge, 1999), pp. 263-78. Good section on *L'Austic.*

Chantal Maréchal (ed.), *In Quest of Marie de France* (Leweston NY, 1992). Interesting collection of essays; apart from Rosenn's, see Emmanuel Mickel's ('Antiquities in Marie's Lais', pp. 123-37) and Robert Stein's ('Desire, social reproduction and Marie's Guigemar', pp. 280-94) on the written textuality of the *Lais*.

Bernadette Masters, *Esthétique et manuscripture: le «moulin à paroles» au moyen âge* (Heidelberg, 1992). Argues that the *Lais* could be a scribal compilation.

Eva Rosenn, 'The sexual and textual politics of Marie's poetics', in
    Maréchal, *Quest*, pp. 225-42. Considers textuality as a gendered theme.
Sarah Spence, *Texts and the Self in the Twelfth Century* (Cambridge, 1996).
    Good chapter on Marie.
Robert S. Sturges, *Medieval Interpretation: Models of Reading Narrative 1100-
    1500* (Carbondale and Edwardsville, 1991). Good chapter on the *Lais'*
    textuality.

4

Compilation and Cyclicity:
The *Renart* and Prose *Lancelot*

Modern books often privilege textual and authorial integrity. There are of course anthologies and collected volumes just as there are multi-volume works, but on the whole we assume that each book contains just one text, which is the work of a single author. Where a book contains more than one text we assume that the rationale for the book is a degree of authorial or thematic unity.

In the Middle Ages the relationship between text and book was more complex. Thus, Marie de France's *Lais*, which in any case are part of a larger compilation, could be seen as a mini-compilation forming a single text with multiple parts rather than as a series of short texts, while, as we have seen, her texts call into question any idea of a single author as point of origin. Although some works nearly always constituted a single volume (notably the Bible, but of course this is originally a multi-author compilation), and any text could be transmitted on its own (this is often the case, for example, with the *Roman de la Rose*), many (if not most) texts became part of compilations. The organisation of compilations sometimes seems haphazard, but from the outset some French literary texts are copied into books that have a clear organising principle (theme, genre, subject matter). Textual and authorial integrity is rarely one of them: thus, for example, the manuscript known as BN *fonds français* 1450 (this is its shelf mark in the Bibliothèque Nationale in Paris) contains all five of Chrétien de Troyes' Arthurian romances in a single sequence, while BN *fonds français* 794 contains four, but both also contain romances by other writers (four and five respectively) and neither book is a 'Chrétien' compilation. More

important to each volume than the authorship of individual texts
is their organisation into a meaningful sequence for the reader:
thus in BN *fonds français* 1450, Chrétien's romances are inserted, in
sequence, as sub-plots into Wace's *Brut* to illustrate the adventures
that took place at Arthur's court in peace time, and the whole
book offers a continuous historical narrative stretching from the
fall of Troy to Britain with minor alterations made to some
romances in order to ensure continuity (see Huot, *Song*). The stories told would be read therefore as subordinate to a larger
narrative made up of texts written by other people. Furthermore,
many medieval writers are aware that their texts will become part
of a compilation and compose their narratives accordingly.
Compilers, then, are merely responding to the narrative dynamics
of the texts they transmit.

This is most obviously the case when a story is presented as an
episode in a longer narrative. This is true, for example, of numerous
chansons de geste: the *Roland* narrates the hero's death, but other
texts narrate what happens before (*Girart de Vienne*) or afterwards
(*Gaydon*); a whole series of texts in the so-called William cycle, all
undoubtedly by different authors and composed at different
points in the twelfth century, deal with the life of William of
Orange or members of his family, with their incessant struggles
against the Saracens and their relations with Charlemagne's hope-
less son Louis (see for example *Les Enfances Guillaume*, *Aliscans*, *Le
Couronnement de Louis*, *Le Charroi de Nîmes*, *La Prise d'Orange*, *Le
Moniage Guillaume*: there are as many as 24 texts in the complete
cycle, but no manuscript contains them all). Romances too are
clearly often episodic: although texts like Béroul's and Thomas'
version of the *Tristan* story were no doubt originally 'complete' in
that they went from the origin of the love affair to the lovers'
death, three shorter texts survive that narrate episodes from the
longer narrative (Marie de France's *Chievrefueil* and the two so-
called *Folie Tristan*, which are different accounts of an episode in
which Tristan feigns to be mad in order to contrive a meeting with
Yseult). Many Arthurian romances present themselves as episodes
in the larger story of Arthur's kingdom, its rise to pre-eminence
and ultimate demise. Two Arthurian knights in particular stimu-

lated a whole series of texts: Lancelot, whose love affair with the queen, as we will see, becomes the subject of an extensive prose cycle of texts, and Gauvain, whose comic philandering and macho posturing lends itself perfectly to repeated plots that narrate his narrow escapes from the clutches of dastardly foes or pining women. The repeated adventures and misadventures of heroes like Gauvain and William of Orange may then be the implicit or explicit model for the parodic *Roman de Renart*, which narrates the misdeeds of Renart the wily fox-knight as he outwits and outrages other members of the animal kingdom in a series of more than 20 *branches* written at different times by different authors, but clearly intended as episodes in the same narrative. Medieval texts are simply not discrete from each other in the way that modern texts often appear to be, bound as they usually are in separate volumes that are then seen as the work of a single author.

Of course, modern texts are less discrete from each other than they might appear since we always read texts in relation to other texts, but what makes medieval texts different is the way they overtly trouble the boundaries that are erected about them. Where does one text end and another begin? And if texts belonging to the same cycle are the work of different writers, but presented continuously, who is actually telling the story? As I suggested in the last 2 chapters, one consequence of written (as opposed to oral) storytelling is the fictionalisation of the author-figure, the supposed story-teller or origin of the tale. The identity and precise role of the author-figure becomes even more problematic in cyclical texts. It is also clear that compilation and cyclicity are inherently *written* as opposed to oral processes: in the oral performance of a story, different episodes of the same narrative or related narratives can never be simultaneously present, as they can in a book.

To compose a text as part of a sequence of other texts by other writers is an obvious way to signal a commitment to a body of narrative material. However, different writers may treat the same material in different ways and broadly speaking there seem to be two modes of compilation and what medievalists sometimes call cyclicity (conceiving of and/or arranging texts as part of a cycle of other texts): repetition and reorientation. This chapter will con-

sider the effects of these two modes and suggest how cyclicity prob-
lematises authorship in medieval texts.

Repetition

A typical Gauvain romance starts with our hero at Arthur's court
and ends when he has returned following a series of often very similar adventures involving damsels that fall in love with him and
dastardly knights who try to imprison or kill him. Sometimes the
damsels are dastardly and the knights well-disposed, but he must
return to court unscathed and unmarried in order to enable
another adventure: Gauvain is a more enduring hero than the
more transitory figures in romance who seem successful in love
and therefore marry, thereby producing narrative closure (an
ostensible resolution to tensions or problems, leading to the end
of the story). Gauvain resists this valiantly. Renart the fox is not
unlike this. He may leave his lair in search of food, or sometimes
just to make his long-suffering foe, Isengrin the wolf, suffer a little
bit more, but whatever happens the status quo will be restored,
since Renart must be ready to leave his lair in fighting spirit the
next time he is hungry, in time for the next episode. Many
medieval narratives do not conform to the pattern of well-made
realist novels, where important changes effected by the plot will
lead to the transformation of the main protagonist, producing a
shift in the status quo so that the end may be represented as some
kind of resolution. Rather than heading towards resolution, texts
like Gauvain romances and *branches* of the *Roman de Renart*
respond to different expectations of story-telling. They do not
move in straight lines, but rather always bring a story full-circle,
ready to start again.

The compulsion to repeat is common in medieval texts,
whether this be formal, as in *laisses similaires* such as those from the
Roland I examined in Chapter 1, or on the level of plot, such as
when Tristan and Yseult repeatedly contrive to see each other
knowing they are likely to be spied upon, as in the episode from
Béroul's *Tristan* that I examined in Chapter 2. In the case of some
texts, the entire narration not only repeats past actions, it antici-

pates future re-enactment of these very same actions. This propensity for repetition is then in turn mirrored by an impulse to retell the story from within the story, setting up a play of mirrors and circularity that is clearly intentional, clearly part of the pleasure of the text. I will illustrate these tendencies first with reference to the *Roman de Renart*.

In the *Roman de Renart*, Renart is able repeatedly to trick the other animals despite the fact that they ought to know better, having been tricked by him in the past. My favourite example occurs in Branche IV known as 'Renart et Isengrin dans le puits'. In this episode, Renart gets caught down a well. When he sees his reflection in the water at the bottom, he thinks it is his wife up to some mischief and climbs into a bucket that is attached to a two-bucket pulley system in order to descend, only to find himself trapped down the well and alone. Isengrin the wolf then shows up and when he sees his reflection with Renart, he thinks his wife Hersent is down the well up to no good with his foe and rival. But Renart persuades Isengrin that both he and Hersent have in fact died and gone to heaven, where food is unbelievably plentiful. Seduced by this account of heavenly abundance, Isengrin repents of his sins before climbing into the second bucket in order to join Renart and his wife. Renart, of course, is already positioned in the first bucket so that Isengrin's weight sends him careering down the well, while Renart is elevated back to ground level.

This episode recalls Renart's past trickery, but it is also notable for its internal repetition. Thus Renart and Isengrin both fall for the same illusion when each takes his own reflection to be his wife. But typically, as soon as Renart understands what has happened to him he turns his newly acquired knowledge of optics to his advantage. Once he has convinced Isengrin of the gastronomic delights that await him in heaven, Renart's strategy for persuading him of the desirability of going down the well involves recalling the reasons for their on-going enmity:

> 'Ceens ne poez vous entrer:
> Paradis est celestiaus,
> Mais n'est mie a touz conmunaus.

> Moult as esté touz jors trichierres,
> Fel et traïtres et boisierres.
> De ta famme m'as mescreü:
> Par Dieu et par sa grant vertu,
> Onc ne li fis desconvenue,
> N'onques par moi ne fu foutue.
> Tu dis que tes filz avoutrai:
> Onques certes nel me pensai.
> Par cel seigneur qui me fist né,
> Or t'en ai dit la vérité.'
>
> (280-92)

('You can't enter here: heaven is celestial, but it is not communal for all to share. You have always been such a cheat, so cruel, treacherous and untrustworthy. You didn't believe me about your wife: by God in all his glory, I never did anything unseemly to her, and never was she fucked by me. You said that I spread rumours about your sons being bastards: but I never even thought such a thing. By the Lord who made me, I am telling you the truth now.')

As usual, of course, Isengrin's greed gets the better of him, despite the fact that Renart reminds him why he should not trust him. Renart recalls here the episode recounted in Branche II (1261-396), in which Isengrin discovers his wife being raped by the foxy fox and afterwards suffers his taunting and mockery. Why should Isengrin believe Renart here when he saw him raping Hersent with his own eyes? He should also know better than to believe Renart's tall story about heaven being located underground rather than in the sky (as a *celestial* place should be) and he should pick up on the irony of Renart's mock modesty when he uses the word *desconvenue* (unseemly), since it is rhymed with the altogether vulgar *foutue*. Fittingly, Renart renarrates his past trickery while plotting his next move, thereby anticipating the imminent repetition of Isengrin's humiliation: as a result of being trapped down the well, the wolf gets a sound beating from the monks who at the beginning of the episode had been chasing Renart.

The compulsion of all the characters in the *Renart* not only to repeat the plot, but to retell the tales of Renart's past iniquities becomes increasingly comic when the other animals are induced to relate his past dirty work while he is in the process of pulling another fast one on them. Thus in trial scenes (which are plentiful throughout the *Renart*), the other animals' accusations become catalogues of Renart's triumphs. In Branche VI, for example, Isengrin is induced to bear witness at length to Renart's misdeeds as Renart denies each of his accusations and Isengrin consequently re-narrates, among other events that make him look stupid, the episodes of the rape and of the well (517-780). Trials are designed to bring Renart's antics (and therefore the story) to an end, but they patently fail to do so not just because he always escapes, thereby evading punishment and closure, but also because they become a means for his story to be retold.

Confessions too would also seem to gesture towards closure: one confesses one's sins in order to repent and bring sin to an end. But when Renart confesses his sins, the account he offers of his wrong-doing quickly turns to bragging as he retells the tales of his exploits all over again. Consider this example from Branche I:

> Renart respont: 'Sire Grinbert,
> Ci a conseil bon et apert,
> Qar se vos di ma confesse
> Devant ce que la mort m'apresse,
> De ce ne pot venir nus max,
> Et, se je muir, si serai sax.
> Or entendez a mes pechez!
> Sire, g'ai esté entechez
> De Hersent la feme Ysengrin;
> Mes je vos en dirai la fin.
> Ele en fu a droit mescreüe,
> Que voirement l'a je fotue.
> Or m'en repent, Dex! moie cope!
> Meinte fois li bati la crope.
> Ysengrin ai ge tant forfet
> Que nel puis neer a nul plet.

Dex mete or m'ame a garison!
Trois foiz l'ai fet metre en prison.
Si vos dirai en queil manere.'

(1023-41)

(Renart replies: 'Sir Grinbert, this is good and timely advice,
for if I confess to you before death strikes me, no evil can
come of this and if I die I will be saved. Now listen to my sins!
Sire, I am blemished because of Hersent, Isengrin's wife: but
I will tell you all about it. She was rightly mistrusted because
I really did fuck her. Oh, how I repent, *mea culpa*! I banged
her many times. I wronged Isengrin so badly that I could not
deny this under oath. May God have mercy on my soul! I had
him caught three times, and I will tell you how I did this.')

And so on for fifty lines. This speech is formally a confession (see
lines 1035 and 1039), but the attention to detail, the crude language, and the insistence on the will to narrate (1032 and 1041)
transform a contrite enumeration of sins into a proud boast.

The most hilarious instance of this repetition and recycling of
narrative through confession comes in Branche VII when Renart
confesses, again in some detail only this time with considerable
punning on the *con* (cunt) and the *fesse* (buttocks) in his own personal version of *con/fess/ion*, to a fowl-priest whom he then eats, as
if ingesting the story he has just told for future re-narration. Such
studied representations of the impulse to repeat (even if they are
playful) suggest a very self-conscious narrative strategy. What are its
effects?

In his brilliant recent book about the *Renart*, James Simpson
argues that the animals' proclivity for retelling the story (through
mechanisms like trials and confession) and also for repeating their
mistakes illustrates the relationship between understanding and
sin, or more accurately a lack of understanding and sin. Of course,
the texts play in this respect on the human qualities of the animal
characters in order to suggest the animal nature of human beings.
As long as people fail, like animals, to understand the nature of
their wrong-doings and weaknesses, they are condemned to live

like animals and endlessly to repeat their mistakes: thus Isengrin allows his greed to get the better of his common sense in the well episode. But lest we take the *Renart* too seriously, we need then to remember that the characters *are* animals, so why should we expect any better of them? The *Renart* thereby offers a serious meditation on the nature of the human condition while drawing us in to an infinitely extensible shaggy dog (or rather shaggy fox!) story.

The Renart's parodic nature makes certain features of its narrative dynamic particularly visible, but an impulse to repeat resulting from a lack of understanding drives many other medieval narratives and their continuations. In the magnificent late twelfth-century *chanson de geste Raoul de Cambrai*, for example, which consists of an original text of some 3500 lines, followed by two continuations that have been joined so as to make one 8500-line text, two formerly united families become locked into a perpetual war of attrition, trading violent deaths in an intense blood-curdling saga that seems only to come to an end when all the characters are dead. Just when peace seems about to break out, the memory of past atrocities rekindles confrontation. Despite signs that the characters had moved on (marriages between the feuding families, holy wars and pilgrimages), that there had been some narrative progression, we are taken back to the murderous rage with which the text began:

> Si con il vinrent es prés sos Origni
> en celle place ou Raous fu ocis
> li cuens B[erniers] fist un pesant sospir.
> Li sor G[eurris] molt bien garde s'en prist;
> il li demande por quoi sospira il.
> 'Ne vos chaut, sire,' B[erniers] li respondi,
> 'que maintenant me tient il au cuer si.'
> 'Jel vue[l] savoir' – ce dist li sor G[uerris].
> 'Jel vos dirai,' B[erniers] li respondi;
> 'ce poise moi quant il vos plait ainsis.
> Il me remenbre de Raooil le marchis
> qui desor lui avoit te[l] orguel pris
> qui a .iiii. contes vaut lor terre tolirr.

Vees ci le leu tot droit ou je l'ocis.'
G[uerris] l'entent, por poi n'anraige vis
mais a sa chiere point de sanblant n'an fit
et neporquant a B[ernier] respondi,
'Par Dieu, vassal, n'estes pas bien apris
qui me remenbres la mort de mes amis.'

(8188-206)

(As they reached the meadows below Origni, Bernier heaved a great sigh on the spot where Raoul was killed. Guerri the Red took good note of it and asks him the reason. 'It is no concern of yours, my lord,' said Bernier, '[to know] what it is that so oppresses my heart just now.' 'I insist on knowing,' came the reply. 'I'll tell you,' said Bernier, 'but I am sorry that you should wish it. I am reminded of Marquis Raoul who was consumed with such pride that he resolved to take the land of four counts for himself. This is the place where I killed him.' Guerri is almost beside himself with rage when he hears this, but his face betrayed nothing of it at all, though he did say to Bernier in reply, 'My God, vassal, you are unwise to remind me of the death of my relatives.')

The story is thereby quickly returned to the scenario of vengeance, which has been repeated continually throughout the text and only temporarily cast aside. It is as if the characters have learned nothing.

A reader's response to repetitive narratives of this kind is not limited to the moral sphere. Such accounts of repeated error do not simply elicit laughter and/or moral condemnation: they are emotive as well. If, as the psychoanalyst Jacques Lacan points out, we are condemned to repeat what we fail to understand, the issue of repetition is psychological as well as ethical: because a trauma is improperly understood it will be endlessly repeated. As the repetition becomes more and more hopelessly bound up in its own logic of repetition (killing to take revenge for a murder can only lead to further killing), repeated mistakes become more rather than less moving as the dimensions of the destructive drive expand infinitely. As the *Renart* seems to have understood, laughter is the only alternative to crying.

Reorientation

If some cyclical texts bring a story back to its beginning, others seek overtly to reorient and thereby appropriate narrative material for a different agenda. A prime instance of this occurs in the vast cycle of romances known as the *Prose Lancelot* and particularly in the two concluding texts *La Queste del Saint Graal* and *La Mort le roi Artu*, generally thought to have been composed in the 1220s.

The genesis of this material is controversial. Some scholars believe that a 'non-cyclical' prose romance – the *Lancelot* – about Lancelot's upbringing, his chivalric exploits and above all his affair with Guinevere, was initially composed independently. Others believe that the two concluding texts (the *Queste* and the *Mort*) were always integral to the cycle. These narrate how the Knights of the Round Table embark on the quest of the holy grail, and, following the completion of the grail quest by Lancelot's saintly son Galahad, how they are then plunged into disarray and fatal discord, first by Guinevere's continued and increasingly public infidelity with Lancelot, then by Arthur's dispute with Mordred, who, it is revealed, is in fact Arthur's incestuous son, not his nephew as had hitherto been thought. Although few believe that any two of these texts (the *Lancelot*, the *Queste*, and the *Mort*) are the work of a single writer (as is claimed in the *Queste* and the *Mort*, as we will see), some scholars believe that the production of the cycle was directed and monitored by a single figure with an overall conception of its architecture. In the large number of surviving manuscripts, the three texts are almost systematically presented as a sequence and sometimes the cycle is expanded further still, particularly by two texts narrating earlier grail adventures and tales of Merlin (*L'Estoire du Graal* and *La Suite de Merlin*).

While the *Lancelot* offers an idealised view of Lancelot and of his relationship with Guinevere, the *Queste* to a certain extent leaves this narrative behind to follow an overtly spiritual agenda, whereas the *Mort* reorients the material yet again to worldly concerns but

offers an apocalyptic vision of the demise of Arthur and his legendary kingdom. If we read both these texts, as they are presented
throughout the Middle Ages, as part of a sequence of texts about
Lancelot, then it emerges that whereas the *Queste* works hard to
condemn Lancelot, the *Mort* works equally hard to redeem him,
though in a worldly, rather than a sacred framework.

The *Queste* opens with the arrival of an unknown damsel at
Camelot. She takes Lancelot away with her to an abbey where they
find Galahad, who is dubbed by Lancelot before returning to
Camelot, where a sword stuck in a stone has appeared with an
inscription saying that only the best knight in the world may remove
it. The court naturally expects this to be Lancelot, but he defers to
Galahad, who also sits in the forbidden *siege perilleux*. While the court
is not looking, an inscription appears on the seat: 'CI EST LI SIEGES
GALAAD' (p. 8) and it is revealed that Galahad is Lancelot's son. The
whole court then witnesses the apparition of the grail, and all the
Knights of the Round Table swear to go on a quest to find it. The rest
of the *Queste* narrates the adventures of the questing knights, particularly Lancelot, Bohort, Perceval, Gauvain and Galahad. Their
adventures are punctuated by assorted hermits, monks and holy
men who interpret each adventure allegorically in order to give it
spiritual significance. Lancelot and Gauvain, however, are gradually
marginalised from the grail quest. There are only three grail
knights: Bohort, Perceval and Galahad. When they find it, they live
for a long time beside it, praying and contemplating it. Finally, after
Jesus himself appears to them, an angel takes Galahad off to heaven
and a divine hand removes the grail. This leaves Bohort and
Perceval to undertake another period of heavy praying, after which
Perceval dies leaving only Bohort to return to court to tell their tale.

From the outset, the *Queste* reorients the material to which it
belongs. The traditional heroes of Arthurian romance, indeed the
heroes of the story so far in the prose *Lancelot*, are subject to criticism, some implicitly, others explicitly. Lancelot, Gauvain, Arthur
and Guinevere are shown, to varying degrees, to be morally flawed.
Thus before the grail quest, Lancelot's epithet has simply been
'the best knight in the world', but a change is signalled by a
prophetic damsel early in the *Queste*.

'Par foi, fet elle, je le vos dirai voiant toz çax de ceste place. Vos estiez hier matin li mieldres chevaliers dou monde; et qui lors vos apelast Lancelot le meillor chevalier de toz, il deist voir: car alors l'estiez vos. Mes qui ore le diroit, len le devroit tenir a mençongier: car meillor i a de vos, et bien est provee chose par l'aventure de ceste espee a quoi vos n'osastes metre la main. Et ce est li changemenz et li muemenz de vostre non.' (pp. 12-13)

('By my faith,' she said, 'I will say this to you in front of all these people here. Yesterday morning you were the best knight in the world: and any one who then called you Lancelot, the best of all knights, was telling the truth, for then you were. But now the person who says this should be considered a liar: for there is better than you, and this is proven by the adventure of this sword, which you did not dare touch. And this constitutes the changing and transformation of your name.')

The transformation of Lancelot's name represents a shift in the perception of the Arthurian world. The damsel's remarks anticipate the repeated, insistent revelation of the inadequacy of the worldly chivalric ideal that Lancelot represents, grounded as it is in his service of Guinevere. As Lancelot himself realises and as he is repeatedly told, his sin is the reason he is excluded from the grail quest:

'... il est einsi que je sui morz de pechié d'une moie dame que je ai amee toute ma vie, et ce est la reine Guenievre, la fame le roi Artus. Ce est cele qui a plenté m'a doné l'or et l'argent et les riches dons que je ai aucune foiz donez as povres chevaliers. Ce est cele qui m'a mis ou grant boban et en la grant hautece ou je sui. Ce est cele por qui amor j'ai faites les granz proeces dont toz li mondes parole. Ce est cele qui m'a fet venir de povreté en richese et de mesaise a toutes les terriannes beneurtez. Mes je sai bien que par cest pechié de li s'est Nostre Sires si durement corociez a moi qu'il le m'a bien mostré puis ersoir.' (p. 66)

('... the sin I have committed with my lady, whom I have
loved all my life, is the death of me, and it is Guinevere, King
Arthur's wife. It is she who gave me vast quantities of gold
and silver and the rich gifts which I have sometimes given to
poor knights. It is she who made me wealthy and raised me
to my present condition. It is for her love that I have undertaken the great deeds of valour of which everyone speaks. It
is she who dragged me from poverty into wealth and from
misery into all worldly happiness. But I indeed know that
because of this sin Our Lord is sorely vexed with me as he
showed me clearly last night.')

The link between Lancelot's sin and worldliness, in the form of
wealth and physical pleasure, is stressed here. From a spiritual
point of view Lancelot's love for Guinevere, hitherto idealised, is
clearly misguided. The hermit whom Lancelot addresses here
makes Lancelot swear to renounce his love for the queen (a
promise he breaks in the *Mort*), but Lancelot's past sins are so
great that he is prevented from successfully completing the grail
quest, thereby demonstrating the inadequacy of the romance
ideal, anchored, like Lancelot's erstwhile epithet, *in the world*.

Like Lancelot, Gauvain similarly flunks the test of the grail
quest. Chastised as a 'chevalier plein de povre foi et de male cre-
ance' (p. 151: faithless and impious knight), Gauvain's
philandering and aimless thirst for adventure seem to be the cause
of his failure to make the grade. As if to signal the disgrace of this
pillar of Arthurian chivalry, his carelessness makes him responsible
for the deaths of several of Arthur's knights. Arthur himself does
not escape implicit criticism, since he opposes the grail quest
(which is from the outset clearly holy) because he realises it means
the end of the Round Table as it had been (pp. 16-17), and once
his knights have departed on the quest, the king is left out of the
story until the end. Like Arthur, Guinevere is none too happy
about the quest (p. 24) putting her own desire to keep Lancelot
with her first. When Lancelot returns to court, it is remarked that
failure in the grail quest is a source of *grant honte* (p. 262: 'great
shame') and we are left with a sense that the surviving characters

are the dregs of Arthurian society, either lacking in the holiness required to complete the quest, or the decency to die in the attempt. What distinguishes the grail knights from all the knights who fail is their chastity, and what distinguishes Galahad from everyone else is his virginity (p. 263), thereby emphasising Lancelot's impiety and lack of chastity. Furthermore, apart from the ubiquitous holy hermits and prophetic damsels, the text is riddled with unmarked Biblical quotation and religious allegory (see Matarasso, *Redemption*). Romance has been hijacked and reoriented.

Initially the *Mort* would seem to continue in the same vein as the *Queste*, since it opens with a discussion of Gauvain's misdeeds on the grail quest as Arthur tries to calculate exactly how many knights he has killed *par mescheance* ('by accident' or 'misfortune'). The *Mort* is certainly a deliberate continuation that signals the fact that it picks up precisely where the *Queste* leaves off. However, it is soon apparent that we have left the spiritual concerns of the *Queste* behind as Lancelot falls back into bad habits with the queen and attention focuses on attempts to catch them red-handed, their attempts to avoid this, and Arthur's persistent unwillingness to believe in their treachery. The *Mort* is a profoundly moving text: unable to resist their compulsions, all the main characters go on relentlessly, but wearily, making the same mistakes well into old age (Guinevere is already in her fifties). And yet the repetition of the *Mort* does not bring us in a full circle back to the adulterous plot of the *Lancelot*, since it is deployed as a riposte to the reorientation of romance enacted by the *Queste*.

Thus far the cycle seems to suggest that if there is something seriously wrong with the Arthurian world, we need look no further than Lancelot and Guinevere's sinful passion. As we have seen, this is certainly the message given out by the *Queste*. Even the *Mort* describes their love as sinful and crazy:

Mes comment que Lancelos se fust tenuz chastement par le conseill del preudome a qui il se fist confés quant il fu en la queste del Seint Graal et eüst del tout renoiee la reïne Guenievre, si comme li contes l'a devisé ça arrieres, si tost

comme il fu venuz a cort, il ne demora pas un mois aprés que
il fu autresi espris et alumez come il avoit onques esté plus
nul jor, si qu'il rencheï el pechié de la reïne autresi comme il
avoit fet autrefoiz. (§4, 1-10)

(But however chastely Lancelot had behaved, following the
advice of the wise man to whom he had confessed when he
was on the quest of the Holy Grail and had totally renounced
queen Guinevere, just as the tale recounted before, as soon
as he had returned to court, not a month had gone by before
he was just as in love and burning with lust as he had ever
been, to such an extent that he fell again into sinful ways with
the queen, as he had done previously.)

The lovers' *pechié* and 'madness' seem to be suggesting to the
reader that as discord resulting from Lancelot and Guinevere's
affair increases, they should be held responsible for the looming
apocalypse. As Arthur himself says: 'plus ne me pooit Lancelos avil-
lier que de moi honnir de ma fame' (§52, 12-13: 'Lancelot could
not insult me more than by shaming me with my wife'). When
Lancelot makes off with Guinevere to save her from being put to
death, despite a temporary uneasy truce, it looks as if a war to end
all wars is to be waged between Arthur and Lancelot. Matters are
not helped by Gauvain, formely Lancelot's favoured companion
and Arthur's nephew, swearing to take vengeance for Lancelot
having killed his brother. Arthur's demise had been announced,
along with the title, in the first paragraph of the text. The weight
of over a thousand pages of narrative seems to point towards
Lancelot as the cause of Arthur's death.

This is not, however, to be. As Gauvain's vendetta against
Lancelot becomes increasingly febrile, Mordred, to whom Arthur
has entrusted Guinevere while he goes off to fight, develops illicit
designs upon her. Arthur kills his monstrous offspring, but is fatally
wounded by him in the process. The shift in focus from Lancelot's
adultery to Arthur's incest and Gauvain's increasing loss of control
contributes to a rehabilitation of Lancelot as the best knight in the
world. When Gauvain is mortally wounded in single combat with

Lancelot, who has repeatedly tried to avoid the confrontation, both Arthur and Gauvain recognise that Lancelot is not to blame. Thus Arthur's parting words to Lancelot are 'A Dieu soiés vous comandés ... qui vous conduise a salveté comme le meillour chevalier que je onques veïsse et le plus courtois' (§157, 52-54: 'I commend you to God and may he guide you safely as the best knight I ever saw, and the most courtly'), thereby implicitly reinstating Lancelot's lost epithet as 'best knight in the world', a point which is reinforced on the very next page when it is remarked that 'Lancelos estoit li mieudres chevaliers del monde' (§158, 58-9). For his part, Gauvain laments not being able to make amends with the one he 'knows to be the best knight in the world' (§165, 16) before he dies and he insists that Arthur ensure a permanent record of Lancelot's rehabilitation:

> 'Sire, ge vos requier que vos me façoiz enterrer a Kamaalot avec mes freres, et vueill estre mis en cele tombe meïsmes ou li cors Gaheriet fu mis; car ce fu li hom del monde que ge plus amai. Et fetes escrivre sus la tombe: CI GIST GAHERIET ET GAUVAINS QUE LANCELOS OCIST PAR L'OUTRAGE GAUVAIN. C'est escrit vueill ge qu'il i soit, si que ge soie blasmez de ma mort si comme j'ai deservi.' (§172, 24-32)

> ('Sire, please have me buried at Camelot with my brothers, and I want to be put in the same tomb as the one in which the body of Gaheriet was placed, for he was the man I loved most in the world. And have written on the tomb: HERE LIES GAHERIET AND GAUVAIN WHOM LANCELOT KILLED BECAUSE OF GAUVAIN'S LACK OF MODERATION. I want this to be written there, so that I might be blamed for my death as I deserve.')

Tellingly, from beyond the grave Gauvain urges Arthur in a dream to summon Lancelot to help him against Mordred, as does an archbishop to whom Arthur confesses. But despite Lancelot's increasingly holy character references, Arthur fails to summon him (something he later regrets, see §186, 41-6), thus making the brutal parricide/infanticide inevitable.

There seems to be no desire here to blacken Arthur's name, as Mordred's incestuous conception is not focused upon in any detail, nor is it even made clear if Arthur knew he was sleeping with his sister. But the fact remains, as Arthur himself acknowledges when he recalls a dream in which he is destroyed by a serpent that issues from his belly (§164), that Arthur's demise is not caused by Lancelot. An important effect of the incest plot is, then, to deflect attention from Lancelot's wrong-doing, to exculpate him. Lancelot dies after all the other main characters, having devoted himself (briefly) to a life of asceticism and prayer. On his tombstone are carved the words '... LANCELOS DEL LAC QUI FU LI MIEUDRES CHEVA- LIERS QUI ONQUES ENTRAST EL ROIAUME DE LOGRES, FORS SEULEMENT GALAAD SON FILL' (§203, 16-19: 'LANCELOT OF THE LAKE, WHO WAS THE BEST KNIGHT WHO EVER VENTURED INTO THE KINGDOM OF LOGRES, EXCEPT FOR HIS SON GALAHAD'). Lancelot is thereby redeemed, but not as a saint (like his son Galahad), rather as a knight. In spite of his sin with Guinevere, Lancelot is reinstated as Arthur's best knight. In other words, the value system according to which his love-service for Guinevere, which inspired him to higher and higher planes of chivalry, is recuperated and endorsed. His wrong- doings pale into insignificance beside Mordred's. If the *Queste* hijacks the *Lancelot* for a sacred agenda, the *Mort* re-appropriates the material and subjects it to further reorientation.

There can be no doubt that this was deliberate. The reorienta- tion signalled by the loss of Lancelot's name at the beginning of the *Queste* is evident. At the beginning of the *Mort*, the end of the *Queste* is pointedly echoed:

> Quant il orent mangié, li rois fist avant venir les clers qui metoient en escrit les aventures aus chevaliers de laienz. Et quant Boorz ot contees les aventures del Seint Graal telles come il les avoit veues, si furent mises en escrit et gardees en l'almiere de Salebieres, dont MESTRE GAUTIER MAP les trest a fere son livre del Seint Graal por l'amor del roi Henri son seignor, qui fist l'estoire translater de latin en françois. Si se test a tant li contes, que plus n'en dist des AVENTURES DEL SEINT GRAAL. (pp. 279-80)

Aprés ce que mestres Gautiers Map ot mis en escrit des *Aventures del Seint Graal* assez soufisanment si com li sembloit, si fu avis au roi Henri son seigneur que ce qu'il avoit fet ne devoit pas soufire, s'il ne ramentevoit la fin de ceus dont il avoit fet devant mention et conment cil morurent dont il avoit amenteües les proesces en son livre; et por ce commença il ceste derrienne partie. Et quant il l'ot ensemble mise, si l'apela *La Mort le Roi Artu.* (§1, 1-10)

(When they had eaten, the king had brought to him the clerks who wrote down the adventures of all the knights who were there. And when Bohort had told of the adventures of the holy grail, just as he had seen them, they were written down too and kept in the library chest at Salisbury, from whence master Walter Map took them to make his book about the holy grail for the love of king Henry his lord, who had the story translated from Latin into French. The story falls silent here and there is no more to be said of the *Adventures of the Holy Grail* ...

After master Walter Map had written as much as he thought appropriate about the *Adventures of the Holy Grail*, king Henry, his lord, thought that what he had done was not enough unless he also told of the end of those he had been talking about and of how the men whose many brave deeds he had recounted in his book died; and for this reason he began this last part. And when he had put it together, he called it *The Death of King Arthur*.)

The way these two texts are spliced together has a number of implications. First, it is clear that although the style of both texts is suggestive of oral delivery (thus the *Queste* 'falls silent' rather than simply coming to an end), both texts are nonetheless clearly written texts, and that the *contes* are conceived as and considered to be constituent parts of a book that draws on other books. Writing is both the origin and destination of story-telling here. The centrality of writing to these texts is reflected in the fact that virtually all the characters are repeatedly portrayed as being able to read.

Indeed on several occasions writing and the ability to read are important catalysts in the plot. For example, at an early stage in the *Mort*, Arthur happens upon his sister Morgan's castle. She maliciously puts him in a room where she once held Lancelot captive, on the walls of which he depicted the story of his love affair with Guinevere, in pictures and then in writing; because Arthur finds the images difficult to believe, he reads the writing in order to authenticate them, thereby suggesting an interesting hierarchy according to which text is more trustworthy than image (§§51-2). But if writing is seen as a source of truth here, this is belied later in the *Mort*, when Mordred uses a forged letter to convince Arthur's subjects that the king has died, thereby seizing control (§135). If the characters see writing as trustworthy and reliable, the text seems to draw attention to its fickleness: it may tell the truth, it may not. This point is underlined, in the *Mort*, by the frequent use of questionable inscriptions on tombstones. Some are simply wrong: for example Gaheriet de Karaheu's tombstone (§67), which is never altered, says Guinevere poisoned him, implying intention and guilt, whereas readers know her to be innocent. Alternatively, other inscriptions have to be modified, for instance the inscription on Gauvain's brother Gaheriet's tombstone originally blamed Lancelot for his death, but it is later altered (§172, 24-32, quoted above) so that Lancelot might be exculpated and Gauvain himself held responsible. This is a world in which writing is central, but where even things written in stone may be altered.

The capacity of writing both to convey the truth and to mislead is thus a central theme of the *Mort* and this must surely affect how we read the writing of the text itself. How reliable and trustworthy is it? If we return to the end of the *Queste* and the beginning of the *Mort*, it is noteworthy that an untruth is proffered. We do not know who wrote either of these texts, but the difference in orientation and style (as noted, the *Queste* has a propensity for allegory, whereas the *Mort* does not) means that they are unlikely to be by the same person. One thing we can be sure of is that neither is the work of Walter Map, who was, as is suggested here, a secretary of Henry II, who died in 1189, whereas both texts have been securely dated as early thirteenth-century, on linguistic and other grounds.

Both texts therefore fictionalise the figure of the author in the text, while the *Mort* may even seek to suggest authorial unity to the entire cycle by remarking in conclusion:

> Si se test ore atant mestre Gautiers Map de l'Estoire *de Lancelot,* car bien a tout mené a fin selonc les choses qui en avindrent, et fenist ci son livre si outreement que aprés ce n'en porroit nus riens conter qui n'en mentist de toutes choses. (§204, 8-13)

> (Now Master Walter Map falls silent about the story of *Lancelot,* since he has brought everything to a conclusion, following events as they happened, and he finishes his book here to the bitter end so that nothing more can be said afterwards which would not be downright lies.)

Again we see here the problem of any sharp distinction between orality and writing in medieval culture as the text refers both to the temporal medium of the spoken word (*ore,* 'now') and to the spatial medium of the book (*ci,* 'here') within the same sentence. This book ends with a claim of authorial unity, truth, and closure, but the authority it thereby constructs is specious if the *Mort* was not written by Walter Map, while the rebuttal of subsequent sequels is disingenuous, since the *Mort* itself is a sequel to a text that also claimed closure.

What we see here is a typical example of how the author-figure in a medieval text is often a fictional figure created by the writer to enhance the credibility of his text. Both the *Queste* and the *Mort* play on the renown of Henry II's court as a centre of learning, and of Walter Map, his famous and learned secretary. The boundaries between the real and textual world are deliberately confused in an attempt to produce verisimilitude. It is therefore crucial not to confuse the fictional author with the writer in a medieval narrative. What we also see here is how aware medieval writers are of the consequences and possibilities of their culture's propensity for rewriting and compilation in relation to the idea of the author. The status of the author is similarly problematic when unfinished (or apparently unfinished) texts are continued by other writers. It is to this question that we will now turn in two of the best known texts of the French Middle Ages.

Selected Reading

La Mort le roi Artu, ed. Jean Frappier, third edition (Geneva, 1964)
Roman de Renart, ed. Jean Dufournet, 2 vols. (Paris, 1985)
La Queste del saint Graal, ed. Albert Pauphilet (Paris, 1923)
Raoul de Cambrai, ed. Sarah Kay, trans. William Kibler (Paris, 1996)

Sylvia Huot, *From Song to Book: the Poetics of Writing in Old French Lyric and Lyrical Narrative Poetry* (Ithaca, 1987). Good introduction to studying manuscript compilations.
———— 'The manuscript context of medieval romance', in *The Cambridge Companion to Medieval Romance*, ed. Roberta L. Krueger (Cambridge, 2000), pp. 60-77.
Pauline Matarasso, *The Redemption of Chivalry: A Study of the Queste del Saint Graal* (Geneva, 1979). Good overall analysis.
Karen Pratt, *La Mort le roi Artu* (London, 2001). Good overall analysis.
James R. Simpson, *Animal Body, Literary Corpus: the Old French 'Roman de Renart'* (Amsterdam, 1996). Witty and stimulating.
Sara Sturm-Maddox and Donald Maddox (eds), *Transtextualities: Of Cycles and Cyclicity in Medieval French Literature* (Binghamton, 1996). Collection of essays on cyclicity; see particularly the Introduction, pp. 1-14.

5

Continuation and Authorship in Chrétien's *Charrete* and the *Roman de la Rose*

Allied to the extremely widespread phenomena of compilation and cyclicity is the equally characteristic tendency for continuations. Famously, Chrétien de Troyes allegedly left two of his Arthurian romances unfinished, but both texts were then continued by other writers. In the case of *Le Chevalier de la Charrete*, the continuation seems to have become a stable part of the text and, as we will see, may in fact be fictional: in other words there is a possiblity at least that the entire text is the work of just one writer, who pretends to have left it unfinished for someone else to continue; we will consider the reasons why he might have chosen to do this. In the case of the *Conte du Graal* several writers produced continuations and no single one became canonical. Equally celebrated is the case of the thirteenth-century *Roman de la Rose*, which consists of an apparently unfinished text of some 4000 lines by one Guillaume de Lorris, followed by a monumental continuation of some 18,000 lines by Jean de Meun. The *Rose* is a particularly instructive text to consider since it is unquestionably the best-known and most widely circulated medieval French text, surviving as it does in some 300 manuscripts and translated into English, Dutch and Italian. Guillaume's 'original' *Rose* seems almost never to have circulated on its own, so the 'original' owes its celebrity to the continuation, and although Jean's continuation eclipsed other attempts to finish Guillaume's text, at least two other continuations were composed. This suggests firstly that continuation was a familiar textual phenomenon for medieval readers, and secondly (as with the *Conte du Graal*) that some texts seem to invite it.

Chrétien's *Charrete*: the work of a phantom continuator?

Chrétien de Troyes' *Chevalier de la Charrete*, which narrates how
Lancelot and Guinevere first come to sleep with each other, opens
with a dedication to his supposed patron Marie de Champagne
(Eleanor of Aquitaine's daughter by Louis VII of France), but concludes famously with a surprising revelation that someone else
finished the text:

> Puis que ma dame de Chanpaigne
> Vialt que romans a feire anpraigne,
> Je l'anprendrai molt volentiers
> Come cil qui est suens antiers
> De quanqu'il puet el monde feire
> Sanz rien de losange avant treire ....
> Del *Chevalier de la charrete*
> Comance Crestïens son livre,
> Matiere et san li done et livre
> La contesse et il s'antremet
> De panser, que gueres n'i met
> Fors sa painne et s'antancïon.

(1-6 and 24-9)

> Seignor, se j'avant an disoie,
> Ce seroit oltre la matire,
> Por ce au definer m'atire,
> Ci faut li romanz an travers.
> Godrefroiz de Leigni, li clers,
> A parfinee la charrete,
> Mes nus hom blasme ne l'an mete
> Se sor Crestïen a ovré,
> Car ç'a il fet par le boen gré
> Crestïen qui le comança.
> Tant en a fet des lors an ça
> Ou Lanceloz fu anmurez,
> Tant con li contes est durez.
> Tant en a fet, n'i vialt plus metre

Ne moins, por le conte malmetre.
Ci faut li romans de Lancelot de la charrete.

(7098-114)

(Since my lady of Champagne wishes me to undertake the composition of a romance, I will do so willingly as one who is entirely hers concerning anything he can do in this world without suggesting any flattery ... Chrétien begins his book about *The Knight of the Cart*, for which the countess gives and bestows upon him the subject matter and the meaning, and he contributes his thought, for he brings nothing to it other than his labour and endeavours.

My Lords, if I said any more I would be exceeding the subject matter and for this reason I draw to a close: here the romance ends crookedly. Godefroy de Lagny, clerk, finished the *Charrete*, and let no one blame him for working after Chrétien, since he did so with the consent of Chrétien, who began it. He composed from the point when Lancelot was imprisoned until the end. He has written so much that he wishes neither to add anything nor take anything away, so as not to spoil the tale. Here ends the romance of Lancelot of the cart.)

This prologue and epilogue have been the subject of considerable speculation on the part of modern critics. Earlier generations of medievalists took the information given here at face value and asked themselves why Chrétien gave up writing the *Charrete*. One common hypothesis is that he would not have chosen himself to compose a text idealising adulterous love, that he only undertook to do so because his patroness imposed the task upon him, hence his remarks about the *matiere* and *san* coming from her (see for example Frappier). According to this hypothesis, in his three complete Arthurian romances (*Erec et Enide*, *Cligès*, on which see Chapter 7, and *Yvain*), Chrétien is an advocate of married love. However, this does not explain why he is as humorous and ironic about his married heroes as he is about Lancelot, nor why he professes deference and obedience to Marie de Champagne in the

prologue, only casually to abandon the story with an indifference
to her wishes verging on insolence. More recently, scholars have
suggested that Godefroy is Chrétien's invention, a narrative con-
ceit to allow him to write about adultery while simultaneously
disavowing it (see for example Hult and Krueger): the process of
continuation is therefore represented here both to comment on
the subject matter (the *matiere* on which so much stress is placed
both in the prologue and the epilogue) by suggesting that the
author abandons it, and to play a joke on the readers and listeners
in that the identity of the author has ostensibly changed in the
course of the text, but without their realising it.

The question of who is speaking is therefore particularly acute. If
Marie dictates the subject matter and the meaning, is the text really
hers? Where exactly does Chrétien give up and Godefroy begin?
Lancelot is imprisoned several times in the romance and so
'Godefroy's' clarification does not help pinpoint the moment of
transition. There are clearly multiple layers of fiction here and this
raises a further question: why accept the authenticity of 'Chrétien'
while questioning that of Godefroy? When the romance was read
aloud to an audience, both 'Chrétien' and 'Godefroy' would have
been absent with the reader referring to both in the third person. It
is easy to think of Chrétien as the 'real' author and Godefroy as a fiction of his confection simply because Chrétien is named in the other
romances attributed to him, but perhaps Chrétien is as much a textual construct as Godefroy (on which see Kay). We know nothing of
either author beyond what we derive from a small corpus of literary
texts. We may choose to believe in one and not the other, both or
neither, but we should remember that whatever we believe is the
result of a choice that is grounded in how we interpret a text.

Once we approach the question of authorship in the *Charrete*,
bearing in mind the possibility that both Chrétien and Godefroy
are fictional author-figures and that we may therefore be dealing
with a *representation* of continuation rather than a genuine continuation, the extent to which the trajectory from one author-figure to
another seems to be imbricated with the hero's and the text's identity becomes apparent. 'Chrétien' announces that his book is to be
called the *Chevalier de la Charrete* and he makes no mention of

Lancelot; 'Godefroy' apparently still calls the text the *Charrete*, but he refers to Lancelot by name. This reflects, of course, the fact that when Lancelot first appears, after a few hundred lines, no one knows his name: he is referred to simply as *le chevalier*, and then as *le chevalier de la charrete*, once he has climbed into the ignominious cart in order to get news of Guinevere's whereabouts from a malicious dwarf. (Guinevere has been kidnapped by the wicked Meleagant; it is explained by the narrator that in Arthurian times a cart was used as a kind of mobile pillory so that to be seen on one was regarded as deeply shameful.) The anonymous knight's name is then revealed by the queen at almost the exact midpoint of the text (3660) during a tournament: the precision-placing of this revelation, which can hardly be random, is a strong argument in favour of the text being conceived primarily as a single written unit.

The hero's dual identity, as Knight of the Cart and as Lancelot, is exploited in a variety of ways. For example, as a means of designating the hero, 'the Knight of the Cart' seems to mean one thing for the readers of the text, another for other characters. The hero accrues prestige with readers because of his willingness to abase himself and endure humiliation, an act which was beneath Gauvain, but he is repeatedly mocked by other characters for having climbed into the cart. The text starts to suggest an uneasy comparison between the hero's love-service, marked as it is by unswerving humility, and Christian devotion (see Topsfield): when entering the land of Gorre where Meleagant holds Guinevere and many other prisoners captive, he cuts his hands and feet on the perilous Sword Bridge, which is suggestive of stigmata, and his rescue of the prisoners is reminiscent of the harrowing of hell. The blasphemous undertones come dangerously close to the surface when the lovers finally consummate their passion:

> Et puis vint au lit la reïne,
> Si l'aore et se li ancline,
> Car an nul cors saint ne croit tant,
> Et la reïne li estant
> Ses braz ancontre, si l'anbrace.
>
> (4651-5)

(And then he came to the queen's bed, he worships her and
bows down before her, for he does not believe as much in any
holy relic, and the queen reaches out to him and embraces
him.)

The text has opened up a variety of perspectives regarding the
hero's behaviour, but 'Chrétien' seems to have invited his readers
to idealise him, before implicitly confronting them with the questionable morality of his actions. Perhaps it is no accident that it is
revealed that the Knight of the Cart is Lancelot *before* he climbs
into bed with the queen. If so, then 'Chrétien' is aligned with the
Knight of the Cart and his pious humility, Godefroy with Lancelot,
the fearless and brave knight who is also an adulterer and the
betrayer of his king, which would reinforce the impression that
'Chrétien' increasingly bows out of this story as he realises where it
is going.

Explicits at the end of texts (non-metrical lines that signal the
end) are usually written by scribes. The *explicit* of two out of six
manuscripts call the text the *Charrete*, but in the manuscript used
in the edition cited here, the title becomes *Lancelot de la Charrete*:
the hero's name has changed in the course of the text, the author
has apparently changed, as has the title. How should we interpret
the title suggested in the *explicit*? With so much uncertainty about
the identity of the narrative voice, about the identity of the hero
and his nature, and about the identity and therefore nature of the
text (assuming a name and a title are supposed to be meaningful),
what we are offered here is a self-conscious use of the role of the
fictional author(s) and of a fictional continuation to generate an
invitation to interpret, as it were an interpretative challenge to the
readers.

The *Roman de la Rose*: the sequel comes first?

Another famous text that plays on a change of title and author
is the *Roman de la Rose*. Here we are probably dealing with a 'real'
continuation: sometime around 1230 a 4000-line poem called
the *Roman de la Rose* (see line 37) was composed, but left unfin-

ished. Some 40 or so years later, the poem was continued and finished by a writer who names his predecessor as Guillaume de Lorris (10530) and himself as Jean de Meun, but in such a way, as we will see, as to render problematic the question of authorship in the poem as a whole. The continuation is some 18,000 lines long.

Guillaume's *Rose* is an allegorical dream narrative in which a figure called Amant (Lover) goes for a walk in a garden, becomes smitten with a rose bud he sees reflected in a pool that is identified as Narcissus' pool, and then interacts with a series of characters such as Venus, Ami (a friend), and La Vieille (an old woman associated with the Rose) as well as with allegorical figures such as Raison, Dangier (which means something like 'hard to get', 'modesty'), Jalousie (a source of some ambiguity, since it is not clear whose jealousy is at issue) and Bel Acueil (Fair Welcome) that are taken to represent different aspects of the Rose's response to the lover. Guillaume's *Rose* breaks off with the Rose locked in Jalousie's castle, watched over by La Vieille. When Jean de Meun takes over, the style changes and Amant is beset by a series of increasingly long mock lectures from a range of allegorical and less allegorical figures: Raison (whose tedious advice Amant rejects), Ami (now an amoral and disabused rake), Amour (whose army is gathered to mount an assault on Jalousie's castle, aided by the dubious figures Faux Semblant and Contrainte Astinence, False Seeming and Forced Abstinence), La Vieille (who turns out to be a game old tart), then finally Nature (who laments man's reluctance to have straight reproductive sex in some detail) and Genius (nature's priest, who offers a rhapsodic exhortation to straight sexual activity in the form of a sermon). The poem concludes with the castle being stormed and a surfeit of penetrative metaphors that can leave the reader in little doubt as to what is supposed to be going on. Indeed the violence of the metaphors (Jalousie's castle is taken by force) suggests rape.

The *Rose* is a complex text, with lengthy excurses and digressions that can sometimes seem tedious to the modern reader. The concentration in critical writing on either its sources or on its rather confused message can obscure just how funny it is: poor

randy, frustrated Amant is treated to a series of lengthy parodic
lectures when basically all he wants to do is pluck his rose as fast
as possible. The allegory itself works through extensive play: for
example, Amant hardly interacts with the Rose at all, but rather
with Bel Acueil, so this apparently homophobic text figures
straight sex through the seduction of a masculine allegorical
figure by another boy. Indeed, sometimes illustrations show two
pretty boys embracing, holding hands or picking flowers together
(see Gaunt). The apparently straight narrative thus turns out to
be unbelievably camp, while the allegorical embodiment of the
Rose alternatively as a castle that one enters through the back
door, or as a sanctuary in which one has to kneel down and kiss
relics at times leaves one uncertain not only as to the gender of
Amant's partner, but also as to whether one is reading about
sodomy or oral sex rather than the vanilla sex that Nature and
Genius seem to encourage. The *Rose* was quite simply the most
successful French text of the Middle Ages and it was well-known
throughout Europe: apart from its wide diffusion, it is frequently
cited and debated by other writers, eliciting in the early fifteenth
century the so-called *Querelle du Roman de la Rose*, in which a
number of well-known Parisian intellectuals took sides for or
against Jean de Meun largely on the basis of his apparently
shocking attitude towards women. It has sometimes been seen as
a compendium of knowledge about love and other matters and its
success has been attributed to this, but its popularity may in fact
derive from its cheeky playfulness, which means that it is open to
widely diverging interpretations. It can be read in bite-size chunks
(and there is plenty of evidence for this in the manuscripts), but
also as a complete text. One thing is clear: Guillaume de Lorris'
Rose becomes an integral part of the conjoined *Rose*. Thus
although a very small number of manuscripts suggest that
Guillaume's poem circulated independently for a while in the
thirteenth century (indeed, as already noted, there are two other
lesser-known surviving attempts to finish it), the success of the
Rose is due to its continuation, thereby interestingly inverting the
hierarchy one might suppose between 'original' and 'sequel'. The
continuation absorbs the original, takes it over completely, but, as

with everything else in the *Rose*, this is done in a playful manner that engages the question of authorship in a sophisticated way while treating it as an hilarious joke.

Jean's text offers an explicit and belittling reading of Guillaume's. When Genius addresses Amour's army with his sermon to exhort the troops to do Nature's work as vigorously as they can, he refers in detail to the garden that Amant entered at the beginning of the poem, portraying it as a namby-pamby place in which people's legitimate sexual urges are deflected and diffused by elaborate courtly rituals. He contrasts this courtly round garden with a vigorous square garden where the occupants' energetic sex is seen as God's work (procreation), setting them thereby on the path to heaven (as I said, the Rose's 'message' is confusing if one takes it seriously). The belittling of Guillaume's garden often takes place through close textual commentary, as for example when Genius comments on the fountain in which Amant first sees the Rose. Genius seems to have the text of the first part of the *Rose* before him and to refer to it directly (for example 20411-28) as he dissects, with biting sarcasm, the earlier portrayal of Narcissus' fountain as dangerous and yet a source of salvation, playing on the common metaphor of love as both illness and cure that Guillaume had used. Whereas Guillaume's lover identified with Narcissus' plight (the point about Narcissus in the Middle Ages being less self-love than the fact that he falls in love with an unobtainable image), here Genius makes no bones about Amant's attraction to the fountain being misguided. He goes on to offer a *fontaine de vie* that is located in his square park as a much better bet and to tell the story of Pygmalion as likewise offering a more satisfactory engagement with loving images than that of Narcissus. Guillaume's allegory is thus systematically examined, interpreted and rewritten here. But why place this thorough-going act of retelling the tale in the mouth of one of the characters? Why should Jean de Meun hold himself at one remove from this act of rewriting?

It is instructive to look at Jean's representation of himself as author in the *Rose*. Amour, the God of Love, names him when he announces Guillaume de Lorris' death:

Gallus, catillus et ovides
Qui bien sorent d'amours trestier,
nous reüssent or bien mestier.
Mais chascuns d'aus gist morz porriz! –
Vez ci Guillaume de Lorriz
Cui jalousie sa contraire
Fait tant d'angoisse et de duel traire
Qu'il est en perill de morir,
Se je ne pens del secorir ...
Car pour ma grace desservir,
Doit il commencier le rommant
Ou seront mis tuit mi commant;
Et jusques la le fournira
Ou il a bel acueill dira
Qui languist ore en la prison
Par douleur et par mesprison:
'Mout sui durement esmaiez
Que entroublie ne m'aiez
Si en ai duel et desconfort;
Jamais n'iert riens qui me confort
Se je per vostre bienvoillance,
Car je n'ai mais ailleurs fiance.'
Ci se reposera Guillaumes
Li cui tombliaus soit plains de baumes,
D'encens, de mirre et d'aloé,
Tant m'a servi, tant m'a loé.
      Puis vendra jehans chopinel,
au cuer jolif, au cors isnel,
Qui naistra sur laire a meun ...
Car quant Guillaumes cessera,
Jehans le continuera
Aprés sa mort, que je ne mente,
Anz trespassez plus de .xl.

                (10526-35, 10552-71, 105591-4)

(Gallus, Catullus and Ovid, who wrote so well about love
would be of great help to us now. But each one of them is

dead and rotting – and here's Guillaume de Lorris, whose enemy Jealousy is causing so much anguish and pain that he is in danger of dying unless I help him ... for in order to deserve my grace, he must begin the romance where all my commands will be written; and he will write it up to the point when Bel Acueil, who is languishing in prison, will say, in his shock and misapprehension: 'I am sorely afraid that you have forgotten me and I am so troubled and have no comfort other than through your good will for I have no other hope'. Guillaume will stop here and may his tomb be full of sweet spice, incense, myrrh and aloe, because he has served and praised me so much. Then Jean Chopinel will come, with the jolly heart and quick wit, he will be born in Meun-sur-Loire ... For when Guillaume stops, Jean will continue it after his death, in truth more than forty years later.)

The narrative play here is extravagant. Future tenses are accumulated in rapid succession to designate events firmly in the real and narrative past: Guillaume will start the text we are reading, but his part is already finished; Jean will take over from Guillaume, but he has already done so; and finally (the ultimate joke) Jean (the writer of these lines) will be born. This passage enabled medieval transmitters to locate the point of transition between the two writers, since lines 10559-64 are an exact quotation of lines 4051-6, and the switch is systematically marked in manuscripts, at least by a rubric, sometimes by an illustration (see the cover of this book). Jean's precision has also enabled modern scholars to date his own composition. But such literary historical considerations deflect attention from the playfulness of the moment. We have been told that the *Rose* is the narration of a dream that had taken place some five years previously, when the dreamer was twenty, and that the dream anticipated a love affair that shortly took place (21-44). If we stick with the logic of the dream narrative, what we are told by Amour is that the dream has been usurped by someone else (a somewhat mind-boggling assertion) and that the text was written by someone not yet born at the time of the narration. To push the joke further, Amour goes on to pray for Jean's safe birth as he is

worried lest something go wrong, which would mean that the
dreamer of the *Rose* would be left languishing, the Rose forever
held captive in Jalousie's castle, the text forever unfinished. The
boundaries between the world portrayed in the text and the world
outside the text are blurred and confused here irredeemably. We
may cling to the biographical information we are given, but it is so
firmly embedded in fiction that it can probably tell us more about
the narrative dynamic of the *Rose* than about its authors (about
whom, in any case, we are told little).

The identification of the author of the first part of the *Rose* as
Guillaume de Lorris rests entirely on this passage. For the modern
reader, therefore, Guillaume owes his identity to Jean, who pre-
sents himself as his predecessor's saviour, stepping in as he does
to ensure Guillaume's story has a happy ending. The successful
outcome of Guillaume's narrative *depends* on Jean's continuation.
As if to further emphasise his precedence over Guillaume, Jean
brings him to life and kills him with the same gesture. His very
name rhymes with *porriz* (rotten) and he is evoked as the final
figure in a list of dead authors, authors (particularly Ovid) on
whom 'Guillaume' himself had drawn in his part of the poem.
Amour goes on to rename Guillaume's book (*livre*) as *Le mireor aus
amoureus* (*The Mirror of Lovers*, 10655) and to beseech his followers
to help 'Guillaume' by helping Jean finish the story:

> Si vous cri merciz jointes paumes
> Que cist las dolereus Guillaumes
> Qui se bien s'est vers moi portez,
> Soit secoruz et confortez;
> Et se pour lui ne vous prioie,
> Certes prier vous en devroie
> Au mains pour jehan alegier,
> Qu'il l'escrive plus de leger.

>   (10661-8)

(I beg you all with my hands together, to help and comfort
poor suffering Guillaume who behaved so well towards me;
and if I do not beseech you on his behalf, then I ought surely

at least to beseech you to give Jean a helping hand, so that he
might write more swiftly.)

Having killed him off, Jean now demotes 'Guillaume' from being
an author to being a mere narrator: Jean is the *writer* here, but the
text is still the story of Guillaume's dream and rather than being
named as an author here (albeit a dead one), he is in fact identified as the narrator in a text by Jean that has quite simply absorbed
anything that preceded it.

But does Jean get the last laugh? One might consider here two
points. First, Jean de Meun may rewrite Guillaume de Lorris and
displace him unceremoniously from his own text, but in so doing
he ties himself to a model that determines the shape of his text: the
Rose remains an allegory of love. However much Jean talks about
other things and transforms the nature of the love that is spoken
about, ultimately the shape of the narrative is dictated by
Guillaume. It may then be significant, and this is my second point,
that the title is always given as the *Roman de la Rose*, that is
Guillaume's title, rather than Jean's. Jean may attempt to take control of this textual material, but some part of it escapes his grasp
and controls him. And lest one place too much reliance on
Amour's words concerning Jean, we should remind ourselves again
of the fictional frame. If Guillaume is cast as the narrator here, the
figure of Jean in Amour's speech is clearly a fictional author-figure
(in that he has not yet been born): the effect of the passage about
the two authors of the *Rose* is that both Guillaume and Jean on one
level are figures in the text not unlike the allegorical figures that
people the landscape of the allegorical garden. 'Guillaume' and
'Jean' are part of the fiction generated by the text, which is not to
say that the *Rose* was not written by two people called Guillaume de
Lorris and Jean de Meun, but rather that we should be careful not
to jump to conclusions about them on the basis of evidence
gleaned from the text. Like Walter Map, Chrétien de Troyes and
Godefroy de Lagny, they should be seen as author-figures within
the fictional frame of the text first and real historical figures
second, at least as far as reading the texts discussed in this chapter
are concerned: thus, for example, manuscript illustrations, such as

the one on the cover of this book, portray them working together, which is clearly impossible if Jean was born after Guillaume died.

The question of who is speaking in the *Rose* is thus deeply problematic: there is a layering of voices and a representation of a layering of voices that in some ways are reminiscent of the layering of texts and voices in Marie de France's *Lais* that I discussed in Chapter 3. The location of the explicit rewriting and reorientation of material from Guillaume's *Rose* in Genius' speech, rather than in the direct discourse of the narrator, is therefore just part of the process of displacement that characterises the *Rose* – and indeed many medieval texts – as a whole. And in any case since the narrator *is* (on one level) none other than Guillaume, the bizarre logic of the text requires that the attack on the garden that Guillaume liked so much must come from someone other than the narrator. But the displacement implicit in the act of continuation also brings both the writer and the reader round in a circle back to the starting point, for it is Jean's attempt to displace and rewrite Guillaume that has preserved him for posterity, and consequently Jean's attempt to kill Guillaume off as author of the *Rose* that gave him life. Freud notes, in his mythologising account of the murder of the authoritarian father by his jealous sons, that it is the act of murder itself that creates the *father-figure* (even as it destroys the biological father), since you can only really be sure of the absolute authority wielded by the father-figure if it elicits the desire to kill him in order to usurp his authority. Amour may try to look forward to Jean's birth and Jean may try to move the *Rose* away from Guillaume's garden, but the *Rose* is always also looking back towards Guillaume, whose authority in some respects derives from Jean's attempt to displace it. Continuation that aims at reorientation can thus lead to a repetition of sorts.

Selected Reading

Chrétien de Troyes: *Le Chevalier de la Charrette*, ed. Charles Méla (Paris, 1992)
Le Roman de la Rose, ed. Armand Strubel (Paris, 1992)

Jean Frappier, *Chrétien de Troyes* (Paris, 1957). Conventional study of Chrétien.

Simon Gaunt, 'Bel Acueil and the improper allegory of the *Roman de la Rose*', *New Medieval Literatures*, 2 (1998), 65-93. Considers allegorical play in the *Rose*.

David Hult, 'Author/narrator/speaker: the voice of authority in Chrétien's *Charrete*', in *Discourses of Authority in Medieval and Renaissance Literature*, ed. Kevin Brownlee and Walter Stephens (Hanover and London, 1989), pp. 76-96. Stimulating study of authorship in Chrétien's *Charrete*.

Sarah Kay, *The Romance of the Rose* (London, 1995). Excellent overall analysis.

————— 'Who was Chrétien de Troyes?', *Arthurian Literature*, 15 (1996), 1-35. Provocative critique of the idea of Chrétien as author.

Roberta L. Krueger, *Women Readers and the Ideology of Gender in Old French Verse Romance* (Cambridge, 1993). Good chapter on Chrétien, including some remarks about authorship in the *Charrete*.

Leslie Topsfield, *Chrétien de Troyes: A Study of the Arthurian Romances* (Cambridge, 1981). Good study of Chrétien, but with a tendency to take the romances too seriously.

6

Revisiting Old Favourites: *Remaniement* in Saints' Lives and the Paris *Roland*

The last two chapters examined cyclicity and continuation in order to call into question, among other things, any straightforward assumptions the modern reader might make about authorship. Figures identified as 'authors' within a text may in fact be more correctly considered 'author-figures' within the fictional frame. A modern author's name is usually printed on the cover of the book by the publisher, who has a legal obligation to identify the writer correctly. The fact that pseudonymous or anonymous publications are the exception rather than the rule only serves to underline the principle: a text's authenticity, authority or appeal is often under-scored and guaranteed by the independently witnessed identity of its author. No such stricture inhibits medieval writers or book pro-ducers: texts may be implausibly attributed to known figures (for example the *Queste* and the *Mort*); or to well-known writers (pre-sumably in order to enhance their appeal); works, including those by well-known writers such as Chrétien, will appear anonymously in some sources; and writers in any case fairly frequently operate under pseudonyms, anonymously or using a name that fails to pro-vide what we would consider a clear identification today (for example 'Chrétien de Troyes', 'Marie de France'). All this suggests an attitude to authorship that is different from our own. In the modern world an author *owns* the text and exercises legal rights over it; in the medieval world an author may claim ownership of a text, but it belongs more to its transmitters and readers than to the person who originally composed it.

A further difference between modern and medieval authorship emerges when one considers our attitudes towards originality. If a modern author borrows material from another writer, he or she is expected to signal the source explicitly. And whereas in the cinema remakes and sequels are relatively common (and sometimes very popular), with written texts we tend to value ostensible originality (ostensible because in fact the plots of most modern novels are pre- dictable, following set patterns and making implicit or explicit use of other texts). In the Middle Ages new plots are certainly devised and valued all the time, but there is a strong and enduring liking for the rehandling (the French term is *remaniement*) of traditional material, or material that becomes traditional by virtue of being reworked. I have already considered several examples of such mate- rial, for instance stories about Roland, Lancelot and Guinevere, or Tristan and Yseult, and I shall be returning to these stories during the course of this and my final chapter.

Some medievalists consider *remaniement* to be an index of orality. Of course oral stories are reworked as they are retold and by defin- ition they do not belong to their originator, even where he or she can be correctly identified. I do not wish to suggest that the written texts that I examine here had no oral antecedents; it is clear that some texts were reworked orally, during and after the period I am considering. But as I have argued throughout this book, the literary traditions of twelfth- and thirteenth-century French-speaking soci- eties were grounded in reading and writing and dependent on books for their dissemination: indeed many early French texts were free translations of Latin texts and therefore necessarily imbued with the practice of rewriting. The phenomenon of *remaniement*, like those of cyclity or continuation, was a demonstrably written practice in that in order to compose new works writers drew on written versions of earlier texts, failing, of course, to distinguish between their own work and their source or sources.

Remaniement in saints' lives

As an illustration of how *remaniement* can work, I will take an example from an important genre I have not so far mentioned:

hagiography or saints' lives. Modern views of medieval literary
tastes are skewed if we neglect the popular genre of hagiography,
since saints' lives were more widely disseminated and appreciated
than the apparently more action-packed or romantically inclined
chansons de geste or romances that dominate modern university
courses. Some saints' lives survive in scores of manuscripts and the
genre contains a surprising variety of racy narratives, ranging from
lurid but popular tales of virgin martyrs (Margaret, Catherine), to
saintly kings (Edward, Edmund), ascetic visionaries (Alexis), married women saints (Elizabeth), heroic warrior saints (George),
incestuous saints (Gregory), repentant whores (Mary the
Egyptian). The saint's life can bring together the conflicting needs
of a profoundly devout society that nonetheless wanted to be
entertained.

The debt of saints' lives to written culture is clear in that early
French saints' lives draw on written Latin sources: learned clerks
relay stories that they read in Latin to the laity in French. But the
move from Latin does not diminish the importance of writing in
the production, dissemination and reception of these texts. As
with romance and *chanson de geste*, the narrators of saints' lives
address an audience of listeners. Frequently they end with a
prayer in which the audience is included, as at the end of one of
earliest Old French texts to have survived, *La Vie de Saint Alexis*
(eleventh-century):

> Aiuns, seignors, cel saint home en memorie,
> Si li preiuns que de toz mals nos tolget.
> En icest siecle nus acat pais e goie,
> Ed en cel altra la plus durable glorie!
> En ipse verbe sin dimes: *Pater noster.*   Amen
>
> (621-5)

(My lords, let us remember this saintly man and pray that he
take us away from all evil. In this world he procured us peace
and joy and the most enduring glory in the other one!
Having said this, let us say: 'Our father'.   Amen.)

Saint Alexis is the story of a young man who, fearful of the sins of the flesh, abandons his wife on their wedding night, encouraging her to devote her life to virginity and God. He travels as a holy pauper, only to return to spend 17 years living under the stairs in his family home as a holy recluse without being recognised. His identity is revealed after his death thanks to a letter he leaves explaining all: his parents, virginal wife and their entourage (including the pope) then engage in lengthy laments at his loss, but rejoicing for his sanctity. Much of this – and their prayers – is conveyed in direct speech. The conclusion thus draws the audience into the prayer that dominates the end of the text, adding their voices to the voices that make up the text itself. The poem derives its force from being voiced and from the implied participation of the audience in that voicing: one can well imagine the audience saying a *pater noster* with the narrator at the end. But if audiences did join in at the end, this is scripted by the written text, which itself has a written text at its centre as the source of knowledge (Alexis' letter). If this and other saints' lives were intended to convey orally narrative material drawn from Latin sources to an audience that did not know Latin, many of whom may have been illiterate, writing nonetheless remains the foundation on which the narrative and the text's narrative technique are built.

A vigorous written tradition of reworking earlier written saints' lives in French quickly develops. There are numerous possible examples; I will offer just one illustration from one of the more popular saints' legends in the Middle Ages: *La Vie de Sainte Marie l'Egyptienne* of which there are over 10 different written versions in medieval French. Mary the Egyptian is, along with Mary Magdalene, one of Christianity's famous repentant whores. After an early life of excessive dissipation – she becomes a whore not from necessity, but because she likes it – Marie has a dramatic conversion and lives as a hermit in the desert for 40 years, before encountering a monk called Zozimas, who becomes the clerical witness to her sanctity (an account of which must, of course, be written down), and to the miraculous circumstances of her death. In the desert she survives on three meagre loaves of bread, while her naked and battered body, together with her unkempt long hair, form a systematic contrast to her erstwhile physical charms. She herself is acutely aware of another important contrast in her story: the difference between her wickedness and the holy virgin's purity, despite their common name. Of course, ultimately Mary the Egyptian resolves this apparent contradition by achieving purity herself, thereby demonstrating a number of important truisms in medieval spirituality: if purity is a state of mind as much as a physical condition, it nonetheless rests on the abnegation and mortification of the flesh.

From the outset (in Latin as well as in French), this narrative material lends itself to different treatments. Some versions are focussed on Mary, others on Zozimas' use of Mary to resolve his own spiritual dilemmas. One widely disseminated twelfth-century version (known as the *T* version), which served as a written source for at least two other versions, is notable for its erotic description of Mary and its colourful account of her youthful exploits on board ship when making the journey from Egypt to Jerusalem, which is where her conversion takes place:

> ... a cel tens, en icel regne
> Ne vit nus hom plus bele feme;
> Ne onc contesse ne roïne
> Nen ot el front plus bele crine.
> Reondes avoit les oreilles,
> Mais blanches erent a merveilles,
> Les iex cler et sosrians,
> Les sorchix noirs et avenans,
> Bouche petite par mesure
> Et pie le regardeüre,
> Le face tenre et coloree,
> Com le rose qui sempre est nee.
> Ja el nés ne el menton
> N'aperceüssiés mesfaichon.
> En som le col blanc com ermine
> Li undoit le bloie crine.
> Les mameles de cele dame
> N'estoit pas menrres d'une pome.

Desous le goule en le poitrine
Ert blanche conme flor d'espine.

(161-80)

(In those days and in that land no one had ever seen such a beautiful woman; no countess or queen had a fairer head of hair. Her ears were round, but they were wondrously white, her eyes were bright and smiling, her eyebrows black and comely, her small mouth perfectly proportioned and her gaze sweet, her complexion clear and fair, just like a budding rose. You could see no imperfection in her nose or chin. Her fair hair billowed around the top of her white neck like ermine. This lady's breasts were not smaller than apples. Beneath her throat, on her chest, they were as white as hawthorn.)

Quant ele vit les hautes ondes
Desmesurees et parfondes
Et ele voit le grant oré
Qui amenoit le tempesté
Li cors de li estoit tant liés
De riens ne cremoit ses pekiés.
Tous les peürex confortoit
Et a joer les envioit;
Car tant l'avoit diale esprise
Toute nuit iert en chemise;
Ele n'iert mie tote le nuit
Nient seuleument en un lit,
Por parfaire a tos ses delis
Aloit le nuit par tous les lis,
Cil le voloient de bon gré
Qui en fisent lor volenté.
Merveille iert d'une feme seule
Ki pooit souffrir si grant foule.

(307-24)

(When she saw the mountainous, frenetic and cavernous waves and sees the great surge the storm brought, her heart was nonetheless so happy that in her sinful state she feared nothing. She comforted all the frightened men and invited them to take their pleasure; for the devil had her so in his grasp that she stayed in her shift all night; nor did she remain all night in just one bed, she went rather from bed to bed throughout the night in order to fulfil all her desires. The men were happy with this and had their way with her. It was a miracle that one woman could take on such a large crowd.)

This version of *Marie l'Egyptienne* has no surviving direct source and although we cannot be certain that these details are the result of its author's initiative, this is at least possible. We can, however, develop a more informed opinion of what writers who were directly borrowing from *T* were doing by comparing the different versions of the text.

For example, passages such as the following demonstrate that Rutebeuf, a prolific thirteenth-century writer who worked in the urban environment of Paris, had a copy of the *T* version before him as he composed his own poem:

> Es le vos entree el chemin
> Devant li vint un pelerin,
> Trois maailes li presenta,
> Trois petis pains en acata.
> Auques fu che de se substance
> Tant com el fu en penitance.
>   Au flun Jordain en va Marie,
> Le nuit i prist herbegerie.
> Bien prés del mostier Saint Jehan,
> Sor le rive del flun Jordan
> Se herbega sans nul ati,
> Un de ses pains menga demi
> But de l'iaue saintefiie.
> Quant en ot but, molt par fu lie.

(*T*, 563-76)

(Here she is on her way and a pilgrim came towards her; she gave him three small coins and bought three small loaves from him. This was all the meagre sustenance she had while she was doing her penance.

Mary goes to the river Jordan and rested there for the night. Near the church of Saint John on the banks of the river Jordan, she rested without any shelter, ate half of one of her loaves and drank some holy water. When she had drunk, she was very happy.)

> Lors encontra .I. pelerin:
> Trois maailles, ce dit l'estoire,
> Li dona por le Roi de gloire.
> Troiz petiz painz en acheta.
> De cex vesqui, plus n'enporta:
> Ce fu toute sa soutenance
> Tant com el fu en penitance.
>   Au flun Jordain en vint Marie.
> La nuit i prit habergerie:
> Au moustier saint Jehan fu prés.
> Sus la rive dont doit aprés
> Passeir le flun a l'andemain.
> Manja la moitié d'un sien pain.
> De l'iaue but saintefiee:
> Quant beü ot, mout en fu liee.
>
> (Rutebeuf, 376-90)

(Then she met a pilgrim: she gave him three small coins for the glory of God, thus says the story, and bought three small loaves from him. She lived on these and took no more away with her. This was all the sustenance she had while she was doing her penance.

Mary came to the river Jordan and rested there for the night; she was near the church of Saint John. On the bank from which the next day she would cross the river, she ate half of one of her loaves. She drank some holy water. When she had drunk, she was very happy.)

Rutebeuf lifts entire lines, indeed sequences of couplets, from the *T* text, but as he reads his source he also rewrites it. This makes the absence, in Rutebeuf's version, of any detailed physical description of Marie seem like a conscious decision on the part of the author: all six complete surviving manuscript versions of *T* have the sensuous description of Marie quoted above. Rutebeuf seems to have hesitated, in a text designed to express his devotion to a saint, to dwell on her physical beauty and erotic charms.

Similarly, Rutebeuf's account of the infamous sea journey from Egypt to the Holy Land lacks the purience that seems to underscore the *T* version and dwells instead on the moral implications of Marie's nautical antics:

> L'Egypcienne est mise en meir.
> Or sunt li mot dur et ameir
> De raconteir sa vie ameire,
> Qu'en la neif ne fu neiz de meire,
> C'il fust de li avoir tenteiz,
> Qu'il n'en feïst ces volenteiz.
> Fornicacion, avoutire,
> Et pis asseiz que ne sai dire,
> Fist en la neif: ce fu sa feste.
> Por orage ne por tempeste
> Ne laissa son voloir a faire
> Ne pechié qui li peüst plaire.
> Ne li soffisoit sanz plus mie
> Des jovenciaux la compaignie:
> Des vieulz et des jones encemble,
> Et des justes, si come moi cemble,
> Se metoit en iteile guise
> Qu'ele en avoit a sa devise.
> Se qu'ele estoit si bele fame
> Faisoit a Dieu perdre mainte arme,
> Qu'ele estoit laz de descevance
> De ce me mervoil sanz doutance
> Quant la meir, qui est nete et pure,
> Souffroit son pechié et s'ordure

Et qu'enfers ne la sorbissoit,
Ou terre, quant de meir issoit.

(131-56)

(The Egyptian woman took to sea: now it is bitter and harsh to tell of her bitter life, for on board this ship there was no mortal man who, if he was tempted to have her, could not have done with her as he wished. She committed fornication, adultery and worse than I can tell you on board the ship: she partied. Neither gale nor storm stopped her doing as she wished and seeking her pleasure in sin. The company of the young men was not enough for her: it seems to me that she contrived to have the old, the young and the righteous men together at her will. Because she was such a beautiful woman she caused God to lose many souls, for she was a deceptive trap. I am indeed amazed that the sea, which is clean and pure, tolerated her sin and filth and that hell did not engulf her, or the land, when she reached it.)

Instead of the febrile image of Marie going from bed to bed, Rutebeuf's account stresses sin and moral decay. His words mark a strong moralising register: *fornicacion, ordure* and *pechié*. He offers powerful images such as hell engulfing sinners. For the writer of *T* the miracle is that Marie can satisfy so many men; for Rutebeuf it is that the sea, 'which is clear and pure', tolerates her vileness. *T* reminds us, in this passage, that Marie is a sinner (312), that she is in thrall to the devil (315), but the tone and content nonetheless betray a prurient interest in her sexual misdemeanours. When we compare this account to Rutebeuf's, *T* seems to have momentarily lost the plot: Rutebeuf, on the other hand, sticks rigidly to a devout moralising agenda.

What this case study suggests is that every act of rewriting is also an act of rereading in that reworking existing material necessarily involves interpretation. This process is fundamental to the modern idea of intertextuality: texts absorb and dialogue with earlier texts, creating an interpretative dynamic between texts and writers that also engages the reader when s/he recognises the intertextual play. In the case I have just examined, it seems likely Rutebeuf worked directly from a written copy of the *T* version of *Marie l'Egyptienne*. However, his readers need not have known the earlier text to appreciate his work, though they would have certainly appreciated it differently if they did. On the other hand, as with other widely disseminated stories (such as Arthurian stories, stories about Roland and so on) readers of any version of *Marie l'Egyptienne* are likely to have already known the plot, so even without the specific intertext of the *T* version, they would have been considering Rutebeuf's account alongside others. There are in fact several different types of intertextuality at work in the production of Old French narratives:

(1) writers reusing or revising existing textual material, which they use fairly closely;
(2) the renarration of a well-known story, but without using existing material closely;
(3) the recasting of a well-known plot.

In the remainder of this chapter I shall consider another example of the revision of existing textual material, in this instance using the more familiar example of the *Chanson de Roland*, before moving on, in my final chapter, to explore the other two forms of intertextuality.

The Paris *Roland* as an interpretation of earlier texts

As the example of Rutebeuf's *Marie l'Egyptienne* shows, writers had no compunction about using other texts as a starting point for their own work. In the case of the *chansons de geste*, the practice of written *remaniement* – as opposed to oral retelling – seems to have led to a lively tradition in the twelfth and thirteenth centuries. The *Chanson de Roland*, for example, seems to have been substantially rewritten at least three times after the version we know as the Oxford *Roland*: whether or not the Oxford *Roland* derives from an oral tradition, in the twelfth century the *Roland* has certainly become a written text and, in at least two instances, a rewriter of the *Roland* is thought to have reworked his material from two separate manuscript versions, choosing the bits he liked best from both. What happens to the *Roland* between 1100 and 1200? I shall take as my point of comparison the so-called Paris *Roland* (so-called because it is preserved in a manuscript that is now in Paris: Bibliothèque nationale 860). I am not suggesting, in making this comparision, that the Paris *Roland* was the result of a direct revision of the Oxford *Roland*. There are at least two intermediary stages of rewriting between the Oxford *Roland* and the Paris *Roland*. Also, it is by no means certain that the text reworked by the writer of the Paris *Roland* was itself derived directly from the Oxford *Roland* since the Oxford *Roland* may have been a *remaniement* of another text that served as a source for the other versions we know. However, as we will see, textual parallels between the Oxford and Paris versions of the *Roland* make it clear that the two are related.

My purpose, in commenting selectively on some of the differences between the Oxford *Roland* and the Paris *Roland* is not to participate in the *Chanson de Roland*'s archeology. There is abundant scholarship charting the poem's transformation as it is transmitted and the recondite nature of this scholarship is hardly of interest to students or general readers, few of whom are likely to read the Paris *Roland*. But it is worth knowing that the Oxford *Roland* is not the only version of the story and in order to understand why it is perhaps helpful to consider the archeological metaphor that is sometimes used by scholars when working on different versions of the same medieval text. The purpose of archeology is usually to strip back the layers (of earth, subsequent building, rubbish and so) that time deposits in order to reconstruct, or produce an accurate picture of what something was originally like. Similarly, the purpose of some textual scholars is to reconstruct the original text from the 'ruins', as they are sometimes called, of manuscript sources (which are always copies, sometimes copies of copies, often also *remaniements*). However, there is a risk in archeology (and in textual scholarship) of discarding as rubbish material that is relevant to the archeology of later periods, material, moreover, that may chart the appreciation and use of the original artefact (or text). Because of the value placed on the Oxford *Roland*, later versions of the poem were disregarded by early scholars, except where they provided evidence to reconstruct or elucidate some part of the great 'original' text, the Oxford *Roland*. But later versions offer important evidence as to how near contemporary audiences enjoyed and thought about the material. I wish, therefore, to look at the Paris *Roland* because it constitutes a different, later (twelfth-century) interpretation of the story, which is given a far more various treatment in the Middle Ages than is evident if one reads only the Oxford *Roland*.

One important transformation is that the material is recast into rhyme: by the end of the twelfth century assonance gave an archaic flavour, whereas rhyme seemed more modern. In addition, key modifications are made to the narrative: Ganelon is a much more dastardly traitor; Roland's fiancée, Aude, has a greater role, accorded for example, lengthy prophetic dreams (see Kay) and suffering the indignity of being lied to about Roland's death in order to spare her feelings; rather than stressing the differences between impetuous Roland and sensible Oliver as the Oxford *Roland* does, the Paris *Roland* sometimes makes them seem like identical twins, stressing the bravery of both and their fundamental similarity (see Gaunt). Compare the following:

> Rollant est proz e Oliver est sage;
> Ambedui unt merveillus vasselage.
> > (Oxford *Roland*, 1093-4)

(Roland is brave and Oliver is wise; both are amazingly worthy.)

> Rollans fu preus et Oliviers li bers,
> Paringal furent et compaignon et per.
> > (Paris *Roland*, 396-7)

(Roland was brave and so was baron Oliver, they were peers, companions and equals.)

The key tension of the text thus is not the conflict between Roland and Oliver about whether or not to blow the horn, but instead becomes the conflict between the two heroes and the traitor Ganelon. (The conflict between Christians and Saracens cannot really be described as *tense*, since regardless of who lives or dies there is no doubt who is right and who is wrong: see line 1015 'Paien unt tort et chrestïens unt dreit', 'pagans are wrong and Christians are right'.)

As well as adding liberally to his source in order to enhance the roles of Ganelon and Aude, the writer of the Paris *Roland* makes innumerable minor revisions to the textual material he borrows, some of which are stylistic, some of which concern details. Some stylistic revisions give a different flavour to the narrative: consider, for example, the use of the past rather than the present tense in the lines just quoted. The Oxford *Roland*'s insistent use of tense switching and the present tense gives the narrative immediacy and, in *laisses similaires* such as those analysed in Chapter 1, the use of tenses combined with repetition give the effect of lyrical stasis. The Paris Roland's use of tense switching is less insistent and if liberal use is still made of the historic present, this is done in a more sustained – and, from a modern perspective, more coherent – way. This means that at high points of the story, we are given a more linear narrative than in the Oxford *Roland*. Consider, for example, the Paris *Roland*'s version of the first horn scene. In the Oxford *Roland*, Oliver's three requests that Roland blow his horn are not differentiated and the repetition gives an impression of simultaneity. In the Paris *Roland*, the first horn scene is textually similar to the first horn scene in the Oxford *Roland*, but the second time Oliver asks Roland to blow his horn, he says: 'Sire compains, car sonez la menée / Que je vos ai hui autre fois rouvée' (348-9: My lord companion, make the signal as I have already asked you to do once today). The third time Oliver says: 'Sire compains, encor voz voil rouver, / Vostre olyfant que le faitez sonner ...' (363-4: My lord companion, I want to ask you again to blow your oliphant ...). We are thus given a linear, rather than a poetic version of events. Indeed, in the second horn scene, Oliver ends up agreeing with

Roland (1698), thereby dissipating the growing poetic tension
that is so powerful in the Oxford *Roland*.

As one might expect in a period of growing literacy (the Paris
Roland was probably composed about 1200), the later version of
the text makes more allusions to writing. Swords frequently have
inscriptions (1582, 2035, 2115, and so on); written sources are
alluded to (in addition to those mentioned in the Oxford *Roland*:
1629-30, 1799); learned clerks with their books are summoned to
interpret Aude's dreams (§§ 295-6: they lie to her!). If the 'oral'
style of the Oxford *Roland* is feigned and contrived, the same textual material has become, by the end of the twelfth century,
stylistically a lot less mannered, and this may well be allied to the
increased importance of writing generally.

To give a fuller sense of the transformations that take place in the
Chanson de Roland as it is rewritten, let us consider the same scene
that I looked at in detail in Chapter 1. To facilitate comparison, material that is more or less identical in the two texts is printed in bold;
material that is similar without being identical is printed in italics:

> Quant Rollans voit que la mors si l'argüe
> **De son visaige a la coulor perdue;**   2610
> Il esgarda, *une bosne a veüe.*
> Durendart hauce, si l'a dedens ferue,
> Et li espée l'a par milieu fandue.
> Rollans l'an trait, a cui la mors argue.
> Quant la voit sainne, touz li sans li remue;   2615
> En une pierre de griez si l'a ferue,
> Si la porfent jusqu'an l'erbe menue.
> Se bien ne la tenist, jamais ne fust veüe.
> **'Deus!' dist li cuens, 'sainte Marie, aiue!**
> *Hé, Durendart, de bonne conneüe,*   2620
> *Quant je vos lais,* grans dolors m'est creüe.
> *Tante bataille aurai de voz vaincue,*
> *Et tantes terres en aurai assaillue*
> **Que or tient Karles a la barbe chenue.**
> Ja Deu ne place qui se mist en la nue,   2625
> *Que mauvais hom vos ait* au flanc pandue!

A mon vivant ne me serez tolue,
Qu'an mon vivant vos ai lonc tans eüe.
Tieus n'iert en France l'absolue.'

Li dus Rollans voit la mort qui l'engraingne;   2630
Tint Durendart, pas ne li fu estraingne,
Grant cop en fiert ou perron de Sartaingne.
Tout le porfant et depiece et degraingne.
Quant Durendars ne ploie ne mehaingne,
Sa dolors tote li espant et engraingne: 2635
'*Hé, Durendart!* com iez de bonne ouvraingne!
Deus ne consent que mauvais hom la teingne!
*Carles estoit enz el val de Moraingne:**
L'angres li dist sans nule demoraingne
Qu'il la donnast au prince de Chastaingne.   2640
Il la me ceinst, n'est drois que il s'en plaigne.'
Et dist Rollans a la chiere grifaingne:
'*J'en ai conquis Anjou et Alemaingne,*
S'en ai conquis et Poitau et Bretaingne
Puille et Calabre et la terre d'Espaingne,   2645
S'en ai conquise et Hongrie et *Poulaingne,*
Constantinnoble qui siet en son demaingne,
Et Monbrinne qui siet en la montaingne,
Et Bierlande prins je et ma compaingne,
Et Engleterre et maint païs estraingne.   2650
Ja Deu ne place, qui tout a en son regne,
De ceste espée que mauvais hom la ceingne,
Mieus voil morir qu'antre païens remaingne,
Et France en ait et dolor et souffraingne.
Ja Deu ne place que ce lor en avaingne!'   2655

Quant Rollans voit que la mors si l'aigrie,
Tint Durendart ou li ors reflambie;
Fiert el perron, que ne l'espargne mie,
Tresqu'en milieu a la pierre tranchie.
Fors est l'espée, *n'est frainte ne brisie.*   2660

---

* The text reads 'Rollans' but this is clearly an error.

Or la regrete et raconte sa vie:
'*Hé, Durendart, de grant sainté* garnie,
Dedens ton poing a moult grant seingnorie.
.I. dent saint Pierre et dou sanc saint Denise,
Dou vestiment i a sainte Marie.   2665
Il n'est pas drois païens t'ait en baillie;
De crestïens dois iestre bien servie.
Mainte bataille aurai de toi fornie,
Et mainte terre conquise et agastie
Que or tient Karles a la barbe florie.   2670
Li empereres en a grant manandie.
Hom qui te porte *ne face coardie.*
Deus ne consente que France en soit honnie!'*

(When Roland sees that death assails him, his face has
drained of colour, he looked about him and saw a rock: he
raises Durendal and strikes the rock with it and the sword has
broken it through the middle. Roland, whom death assails,
withdraws it. When he sees it still whole, he nearly loses his
mind; he struck a hard rock with it and cleaves it in two
through to the grass underneath. No one had ever seen him
hold his sword more firmly. 'God!', said the count, 'Holy
Mary, help me! Alas, renowned Durendal, as I leave you I am
increasingly sorrowful. I will have won so many battles with
you and attacked so many lands that Charles with the white
beard now controls. May it please God, who sits up in the
clouds, that you never hang at the side of an unworthy man!
You will never be taken from me while I am alive, for I have
had you a good long time. There will never be another such
sword in holy France.'

Duke Roland sees death cruelly besetting him; he held
Durendal, which he knew so well, and struck a mighty blow
on a Cerdagne stone. He cleaves it in two, breaks and shatters
it. When Durendal neither bends nor breaks, his pain
spreads throughout his body and increases. 'Alas, Durendal,

* This line has been moved.

you are of such fine craftsmanship! May God never allow any
unworthy man to hold you! Charles was in the valley of
Mauritania: an angel told him that without delay he should
give it to the prince of Chastaingne. He girded it on me and
it is not right that he should complain of this.' And Roland
with the fearsome countenance said: 'I conquered with it
Anjou and Germany and I conquered with it Poitou and
Britanny, Pulia and Calabria and all Spain, I conquered with
it Hungary and Poland, Constantinople, which sits in its
domain, and Monbrin which is situated in the mountains,
and I took together with my men Ireland, and England and
many strange lands. May it never please God, who has everything in his power, that an unworthy man gird this sword! I
would rather die than let it remain among pagans and cause
France to be sorrowful and in deep anguish because of this;
may it never please God that this happen!'

When Roland sees that death torments him so, he holds
Durendal with its glittering gold; he strikes the rock and does
not spare it, cleaving the stone in two. The sword bounces
back: it is neither broken nor shattered. Now he laments for
it and recalls his life: 'Alas, Durendal, endowed with great
sanctity, there is great power in your hilt: a tooth from Saint
Peter and blood from Saint Denis, and there is some of holy
Mary's clothing. It is not right that a pagan should wield you;
you should be served by Christians. I will have fought many
battles with you, conquered and lain to waste many lands that
white-bearded Charles now controls. The emperor has a
mighty household. Let no man who bears you ever behave in
a cowardly manner. Let God not allow France to be shamed
by this.')

The fact that some lines are identical while others show strong sim-
ilarities to parallel lines in the Oxford *Roland* indicates, as already
noted, that the Paris *Roland* either derives from a similar version,
or at the very least that they share a common source. How has the
remanieur responsible for this scene in the Paris *Roland* interpreted
the material?

The most striking difference between the Oxford and Paris versions of this scene is that whereas Durendal fails to shatter, but bounces off the rock in the earlier version of the text, in the later version Durendal cleaves a series of rocks in two. The effect is to reinforce the sense of Durendal's indestructibility and thereby Roland's worth: not only is he unable to break the sword, but in his attempt to do so he shatters rock, nature's hardest material. Even as he dies Roland's strength is thus portrayed as super-human.

A further difference is that the Paris text stresses Roland's dying wish that Durendal not pass into the hands of a vile man. In the Oxford *Roland*, the hero first declares that he does not wish a man who flees to have Durendal (2309), then he expresses the rather vague wish that Durendal not remain among the Saracens (2336), and finally he says that he wants no cowardly man to have his sword (2351). In the Paris *Roland*, line 2309 is adapted and the term *mauvais hom* is used (2626), to be picked up in line 2652, which has no direct equivalent in the Oxford *Roland*. Line 2672, in the third *laisse*, then echoes line 2351, but the effect is different given the repetition of *mauvais hom* in the first two *laisses* that make up the triptych. It should be remembered that immediately before these *laisses similaires*, a Saracen has (unsuccessfully) attempted to take Durendal away from Roland and that his speeches here are a response to this. The three *laisses* in the Paris *Roland* cohere, then, better with the narrative context than the three *laisses* in the Oxford *Roland*, which are more concerned with the immediate, internal poetic effect of the scene. When this is considered alongside the Paris *Roland*'s dual focus on Durendal's indestructibility *and* Roland's superhuman strength, a sustained process of rewriting – and interpretation – emerges.

It is striking that both the examples examined in this chapter interpret earlier texts, but that in so doing they eliminate ambiguity: Rutebeuf avoids the problems posed by sensuality; the Paris *Roland* offers a much more unequivocal presentation of Roland's strength (and elsewhere in the text of Roland and Oliver's relationship, Ganelon's treachery, Aude's plight and so on). By contrast, the type of intertextuality I shall examine in my final chapter almost invariably opens up narrative material to play.

Selected Reading

Les Textes de la Chanson de Roland: Tome VI: Le Texte de Paris, ed. Raoul Mortier (Paris, 1942)

Rutebeuf: Oeuvres complètes, ed. Michel Zink, 2 vols. (Paris, 1989)

La Vie de Saint Alexis, ed. C. Storey (Oxford, 1946)

La Vie de Sainte Marie l'Egyptienne: versions en ancien et en moyen français, ed. Peter Dembowski (Geneva, 1977)

Simon Gaunt, *Gender and Genre in Medieval French Literature* (Cambridge, 1995). For more on the Paris *Roland* and *Marie l'Egyptienne*.

Sarah Kay, *The Chansons de Geste in the Age of Romance: Political Fictions* (Oxford, 1995). Stimulating study of the *chansons de geste*, including many later texts like the Paris *Roland*.

Duncan Robertson, *The Medieval Saints' Lives: Spiritual Renewal in Old French Literature* (Nicholasville KY, 1998). Good general study of Old French hagiography.

Judith Still and Michael Worton, 'Introduction', in *Intertextuality: Theories and Practice*, ed. Still and Worton (Manchester and New York, 1990), pp. 1-44. Good introduction to the theory of intertextuality.

7

Debating Tristan: Béroul, Thomas and Chrétien

Close textual parallels between *remaniements* and earlier versions of *chansons de geste* and hagiography suggest that writers were working from written sources. Somewhat paradoxically, in that romance is often thought to partake more of written culture than either *chansons de geste* or saints' lives, the appropriation of other writers' material is unusual in the romance tradition. Romance writers frequently, however, chose to rework a popular tale, the most common examples being the great love stories of Tristan and Yseult and Lancelot and Guinevere.

In Chapters 4 and 5, I examined Chrétien de Troyes' *Charrete* and parts of the prose-Lancelot which rework earlier French sources, now lost. Here I wish to focus on stories about Tristan. In the twelfth century there were at least two full-length verse romances in French about Tristan and Yseult in circulation, though both survive now in only fragmentary form: Béroul's, and another by Thomas of Britain. I suggested in Chapter 2 that Béroul's *Tristan* is a written text that aims to give the impression of oral story-telling. I also drew attention to the way Béroul sets his version within an intertextual framework, in that he draws attention to other versions (see pp. 45-6). By inviting comparison between his version and others, Béroul contrasts his interpretation of the story with others. Significantly, Thomas does precisely the same thing.

Thomas and Béroul: lovers or sinners?

Towards the end of Thomas' romance, Tristan is in exile with his brother-in-law Kaherdin. He is shortly to be approached by

another Tristan, nick-named the Dwarf, who asks for help in res-
cuing his abducted wife. In helping the Dwarf, old battle wounds
are opened and exacerbated for Tristan: as a young man he had
been wounded by Yseult's supernatural uncle, the Morholt, and
only Yseult has the supernatural knowledge to cure him. In
Thomas' version of the story, Kaherdin goes to England in disguise
to fetch Yseult, but before launching into all this, Thomas evokes
another version in which Kaherdin is the abductor of the Dwarf's
wife and Governal (Tristan's mentor) the messenger:

> Seignurs, cest cunte est mult divers,
> E pur ço l'uni par mes vers
> E di en tant cum est mester
> E le surplus voil relesser.
> Ne vol pas trop en uni dire:
> Ici diverse la matyre.
> Entre ceus qui solent cunter
> E del cunte Tristran parler,
> Il en cuntent diversement:
> Oï en ai de plusur gent.
> Asez sai que chescun en dit
> E ço que il unt mis en escrit,
> Mes sulun ço que j'ai oï,
> Nel dïent pas sulun Breri
> Ky solt les gestes e les cuntes
> De tuz les reis, de tuz les cuntes
> Ki orent esté en Bretaingne.
> Ensurquetut de cest' ovraingne
> Plusurs de noz granter ne volent
> Ço que del naim dire ci solent,
> Que femme Kaherdin dut amer:
> Li naim redut Tristran navrer
> E entuscher par grant engin,
> Quant ot afolé Kaherdin;
> Pur ceste plaie e pur cest mal
> Enveiad Tristan Guvernal
> En Engleterre pur Ysolt.

Thomas iço granter ne volt,
E si volt par raisun mustrer
Qu'iço ne put pas esteer.
Cist fust par tut la part coneü
E par tut le regne seü
Que de l'amur ert parçuners
E emvers Ysolt messagers.
Li reis l'en haeit mult forment,
Guaitier le feseit a sa gent:
E coment pust il dunc venir
Sun servise a la curt offrir
Al rei, as baruns, as serjanz,
Cum fust estrange marchanz,
Que hum issi coneüz
N'i fud mult tost aparceüz?
Ne sai coment il se gardast,
Ne coment Ysolt amenast.
Il sunt del cunte forsveié
E de la verur esluingné,
E se de ço ne volent granter,
Ne voil vers eus estriver;
Tengent le lur e jo le men:
La raisun s'i pruvera ben!

(Douce fragment, 837-86)

(My lords, there are many versions of this story, and for this
reason I bring it together in my poem, saying as much as is
necessary and leaving the rest. But I do not wish to bring it
together too much: here there are different accounts of what
happened. Among those who tell stories and relate the story
of Tristan, there are different versions: I have heard various
ones from different people. I know what each one says and
what they have written down, but according to what I have
heard, they do not follow Breri, who knew all the legends and
tales of all the kings and all the counts who used to live in
Britanny. Above all, in relation to the matter in hand, some do
not wish to concede to us what is said about the Dwarf, whose

wife is supposed to have loved Kaherdin: the Dwarf is said to have wounded Tristan and to have poisoned him treacherously, after confounding Kaherdin; because of this wound and illness Tristan would have sent Governal to England for Yseult. Thomas cannot agree with this, and wishes to demonstrate through reason that it cannot be so. He [Governal] was known everywhere and throughout the realm he was known to be an accomplice in [Tristan's] love and a messenger to Yseult. The king hated him intensely for this and had his men on the look out for him: and how could he have come to offer his service at court, to the king, his barons and sergeants as if he were a foreign merchant, without such a well-known figure being quickly recognised? I do not know how he could have prevented this, nor how he could have taken Yseult off with him. These other story-tellers have deviated from the story and left the truth behind, and if they do not wish to concede this, I do not wish to argue it out with them. They can have their version and I mine: reason will prove who is right!)

Thomas' interjection makes it clear that he expects his audience to know the story – and the detail of what is about to happen – already. He explicitly sets his version in the context of a dialogue between different story-tellers, involving diverging interpretations. As Mark Chinca has argued, it is telling that Thomas appeals to reason and verisimilitude (plausible realism) to defend his version: despite the story's supernatural elements, he wishes his version to be read in relation to real life, his rhetorical questions suggesting that other writers stretch the bounds of credibility to and beyond their limits. Like Béroul, Thomas implicitly acknowledges that his text is one *remaniement* among others when he evokes other versions in order to trash them and promote the authenticity of his own on the grounds that it derives from a superior source.

This engagement with other versions by both Béroul and Thomas is significant when it is considered that the two writers offer such different interpretations of the material. With deft, even dodgy logic, Béroul uses the magic potion that has caused the star-crossed pair to fall in love to exculpate the lovers: because their

love is involuntary, they are not responsible for their actions. As
Yseult says to the hermit Ogrin:

> 'Sire, por Deu omnipotent,
> Il ne m'aime pas, ne je lui,
> Fors par un herbé dont je bui,
> Et il en but; ce fu pechiez.
> Por ce nos a li rois chaciez.'
>
> (1412-16)

('My lord, by almighty God, he does not love me, nor I him,
were it not for a potion I drank and which he drank too; it
was a sin. This is why the king has exiled us.)

Playing on contemporary theological debates about intention and
sin (see Hunt), Béroul seems to imply that because the lovers' 'sin'
is accidental they are less blameworthy.

Thomas, on the other hand, makes no attempt to excuse the
lovers. He is given to moralising digressions:

> Oez merveilluse aventure,
> Cum genz sunt d'estrange nature,
> Que en nul lieu ne sunt estable:
> De nature sunt si changable,
> Lor mal us ne poent laissier,
> Mais le buen puent changer.
> El mal si acostomer sont,
> Que pur dreit us tuit dis l'unt,
> E tant usent la colvertise
> Qu'il ne sevent qu'est franchise,
> E tant demainent vilanie
> Qu'il oblient corteisie;
> De malveisté tant par se painent
> Que tute lor vie laenz mainent,
> De mal ne se puent oster,
> Itant se solent aüser.
>
> (Sneyd 1 fragment, 234-49)

(Listen to an amazing tale, how human nature is strange, for people are fickle: they are changeable by nature, cannot give up their wicked ways, but are able to change good habits. They are so used to evil that they all confuse it with goodness, and they are so given to wickedness that they do not know what honesty is and they so are so vilainous that they forget courtesy; they are so devoted to badness that they reside with it throughout their lives. They cannot renounce evil, because they become so used to it.)

This diatribe, which lasts another 50 lines, precedes Tristan's decision to take a wife in order to lessen the pain of Yseult being married to his uncle. We are being warned to question Tristan's actions here, which indeed turn out to be questionable: he marries another woman called Yseult (thinking this might help him live without the queen), but fails to consummate the marriage when he recalls his true love.

Béroul and Thomas also adopt different styles. As we saw in Chapter 2, Béroul fosters an impression of oral immediacy. His narrator is intensely engaged with the story and expresses his sympathies openly at every opportunity. There is little analysis on the part of the narrator; he concentrates rather on physical detail, direct speech and opinionated interjections. Thomas has a more analytic, overtly clerical narrative style. He enjoys contorted, playful and deliberately confusing accounts of the characters' motivation, as when Tristan is deciding on marriage to the second Yseult:

> Tristran quida Ysolt gurpir
> E l'amur de sun cuer tolir;
> Par espuser l'altre Ysolt,
> D'iceste delivrer se volt;
> E si ceste Ysolt ne fust,
> L'altre itant amé ne oüst;
> Mais par iço qu'Isol amat
> D'Ysol amer grant corage ad;
> Mais par iço qu'il ne volt lassier

Ad il vers ceste le voleir,
Car s'il poüst aveir la reïne
Il n'amast Ysolt la meschine:
Pur ço dei jo, m'est avis, dire
Que ço ne fut amur ne ire;
Car si ço fin' amur fust,
La meschine amé ne oüst
Cuntre volenté s'amie;
Dreite haür ne fu ço mie,
Car pur l'amur la reïne
Enama Tristrans la meschine;
E quant l'espusa pur s'amur,
Idunc ne fu ço pas haür;
Car s'il de cuer Ysolt haïst
Ysolt pur s'amur ne presist,
Se de fin' amur l'amast
L'altre Ysolt nen espusast.

(306-31)

(Tristan thought he could leave Yseult and remove love from his heart; he wants to give up this one by marrying the other Yseult; and without one Yseult he would not have loved the other so much; but because he loved Yseult he wishes to love Yseult; but because he does not wish to give up [his love] he wants this one, for if he could have had the queen, he would not have loved the maiden Yseult: this is why I think I must say that he was motivated by neither love nor anger; for if it had been pure love, he would not have loved the maiden against the wishes of his lover; nor was it pure hatred for Tristan became infatuated with the maiden for the queen's love; and when he married her for love, this then was not hatred; for if he had hated Yseult in his heart he could not have wanted Yseult for her love; if he had loved with pure love, he could not have married the other Yseult.)

It is difficult to keep track of which Yseult is which and whose love motivates Tristan's marriage (*s'amur* in 326 and 329 could be his or her love). But lurking in Thomas' ludic rhetoric, not once but twice, is the contention that Tristan's love for Yseult is not pure love (lines 320 and 330). If it follows, then, that his love is impure, we are being invited once again to dwell on the moral implications of the lovers' actions.

In the lengthy monologue that follows, Tristan's moral confusion is revealed in all its messiness (412-589), as he decides it would be a 'sin' if he slept with his wife and broke 'faith' with Yseult, his uncle's wife:

> Ma fei ment a Ysolt m'amie
> Se d'altre ai delit en ma vie
> E si d'iceste mei desport
> Dunc frai pechié e mal e tort.
>
> (440-3)

(If I ever take pleasure with another, I break faith with my lover Yseult, and thus if I sleep with this woman, I will commit a sin and do wrong and something bad.)

Thomas' text probably predates Béroul's and we do not know if Béroul knew Thomas' version. We cannot, therefore, suppose a specific intertextual dialogue about the nature of sin. On the other hand, an understanding of sin will be integral to any interpretation of the Tristan story, pointing up divergent understandings of the couple's actions.

Thomas' *Tristan* must originally have been over 20,000 lines long; unfortunately only 3000 or so lines have survived in eight fragments (one was recently discovered). We can deduce a lot from these fragments, however, about the tone and style of the text. Thomas' conclusion supports the view that he had a moralising agenda:

> Tumas fine ci sun escrit:
> A tuz amanz saluz i dit,
> As pensis e as amerus,
> As emvius, as desirus,

As enveisiez e as purvers,
[A tuz cels] ki orunt ces vers.
[S]i dit n'ai a tuz lor voleir,
[Le] milz ai dit a mun poeir,
[E dit ai] tute la verur,
[Si cum] jo pramis al primur.
E dis e vers i ai retrait:
Pur essample issi ai fait
Pur l'estorie embelir,
Que as amanz deive plaisir,
E que par lieus poissent troveir
Choses u se puissent recorder:
Aveir em poissent grant confort,
Encuntre change, encontre tort,
Encuntre paine, encuntre dolur,
Encuntre tuiz engins d'amur!

                      (Sneyd 2 fragment, 38-57)

(Thomas finishes writing here; he greets all lovers, the pen-
sive and loving, the jealous and lusty, the hedonists and
perverts, all those who will hear this poem. If I have not
spoken according to the wishes of all, I have done my best
and told the whole truth just as I promised when I started.
And I have composed many sentences and verses: I have
done this to offer an example in order to embellish the story,
which lovers should enjoy, finding things to remember for
contemplation: they can take great comfort in the face of
fickleness, of wrong-doing, of pain and sorrow, in the face of
all love's deceptions.)

The term *essample*, the French equivalent of the Latin *exemplum*, is
revealing here: an *exemplum* is a story told with an explicit moral
point. It is also noteworthy that Thomas does not expect all his
readers to approve of his work (44), even though he has told the
truth. This is hardly surprising. Why should lovers take comfort
(54) in a story that ends in the death of the hero and heroine? And
why do so many of the adjectives Thomas uses to characterise

lovers have an overwhelmingly negative resonance?

If Thomas' overall interpretation was critical of the lovers (see Hunt), it seems odd that he devotes so much time, so many words, to retelling a tale of which at some level he disapproved. Béroul obviously loved to love the lovers and it is easy to understand why he wanted to write a *Roman de Tristan*. Thomas' motivation is less clear. He seems both attracted and repelled by the material. But this is quite typical of some courtly writers: consider Chrétien de Troyes' equivocal attitude towards Lancelot in the *Charrete*. The point is that courtly culture is less interested in an idealising portrait of *fin' amour* than in engendering a debate about love, what it was, the problems it brings, the moral questions it poses, whether it is possible in the real world, and so on. Retelling traditional stories was a prime vehicle for this debate.

Thickening the plot: Chrétien's *Cligès*

The Tristan story was one of the most enduring of the Middle Ages and part of its appeal was undoubtedly its susceptibility to different interpretations. Were the lovers right or wrong? Does love absolve individuals of moral responsibility? Does all-consuming, uncontrollable love, as symbolised by the magic potion, happen in the real world? And if it does, should we discard our usual sense of morality to condone adultery, or even, by medieval standards, incest (given Yseult is Tristan's uncle's wife)? Debate and dialogue around issues such as these were not, however, confined to texts that explicitly retell the story of Tristan and Yseult, for numerous other texts invite us to read love stories in relation to the Tristan narrative.

This is most obviously the case with texts about Lancelot and Guinevere, for both plots involve a queen's adultery. *La Mort le roi Artu*, for instance, makes an explicit reference to Tristan when Lancelot's cousin, Bohort, pleads with the queen on Lancelot's behalf. She believes he loves another and Bohort tries to persuade her to look kindly upon Lancelot by citing, from *la veroie estoire* (the true text), examples of men who have come to a bad end because of love. After Samson, Hector and Achilles, comes Tristan:

Et a nostre tens meïsmes, n'a pas encore cinc anz que
Tristans en morut, li niés au roi Marc, qui si loiaument ama
Yseut la blonde que onques en son vivant n'avoit mespris vers
lui. Que en diroie ge plus? Onques nus hom ne s'i prist fer-
mement qui n'en moreust (§ 59, 54-60)

(And even in our time, not even five years ago, Tristan, king
Mark's nephew, who loved Yseult the Blond so much that he
never did her any wrong, died of this. What more can I say?
No man ever loved so truly without dying of this.)

Bohort's logic is questionable: he seems to imply that true lovers
come to a bad end when they pursue their desires, but that Lancelot
will come to a bad end *anyway* if Guinevere spurns him. He concludes that unless Guinevere loves Lancelot he will pine away, which
would be a tragedy for society at large because he is such a great
knight (§ 59, 79-84). However, this discreetly draws a veil over the
fact that adultery with the queen is a treasonable offence that potentially damages the kingdom more profoundly than the loss of just
one knight, however great. The explicit reference to Tristan and
Yseult, however, invites us to see parallels between the two plots and
to interpret accordingly: whatever Lancelot and Guinevere's qualities, their actions are hardly legitimate.

Invitations to read texts about Lancelot and Guinevere in relation to the Tristan story are not always this explicit. In Chrétien's
Charrete, for example, one scene strongly recalls a scene from
Tristan. After the lovers spend the night together, wicked
Meleagant, the queen's abductor, whom Lancelot slays in the final
scene, realises that someone has been in her bed because of tell-
tale traces of blood from Lancelot's wounds. Not realising that
Lancelot has entered the chamber through the window (because
it is barred), Meleagant accuses her of sleeping with Kay the
seneschal, who is nearby, because he still has wounds that have not
healed. This leads Lancelot to leap to Guinevere's defence, taking
a carefully worded judicial oath according to which he swears that
Kay did not spend the night with the queen. All this recalls the
episode from Béroul's *Tristan* I examined in Chapter 2, in which

Tristan leaves traces of blood beside the queen's bed, thereby giving his enemies evidence of his treachery. The parallels do not just concern the situation as there are also textual echoes. When accusing Guinevere, Meleagant calls the blood 'ansaignes bien veraies' (4774: true signs), while in *Tristan* the treacherous dwarf who has entrapped the lovers calls the blood 'veraie enseigne' (778: a true sign). Furthermore, Lancelot's judicial oath parallels a subsequent episode in *Tristan* when Yseult takes a carefully staged ambiguous judicial oath before King Arthur's court in order to proclaim her innocence. She agrees to take the oath, but only in a place she designates, which happens to be near a bog. She has Tristan disguise himself as a filthy beggar and then, in front of the whole court, she rides across the bog on his back. She is then able to swear that no man has ever been between her legs except for her husband the king, and the beggar who gave her the piggy-back: the court is duly impressed by how scrupulous her oath is. Like Lancelot in the *Charrete*, she is able simultaneously to tell the truth and mislead. Béroul's *Tristan* was probably written after the *Charrete*, but a precise sequence and chronology is not necessary to discern intertextual play here, since we do know that Tristan stories were circulating at the time when Chrétien wrote his romances: not only does Thomas' *Tristan* predate Chrétien's romances, but Chrétien himself makes several explicit references to Tristan and Yseult, though like Thomas he takes a critical view of the lovers' behaviour.

This is quite explicit in one of the lyric poems attributed to him:

> Onques du buvrage ne bui
> Dont Tristan fu enpoisonnez;
> Mes plus me fet amer que lui
> Fins cuers et bone volentez.
> Bien en doit estre miens li grez,
> Qu'ainz de riens efforciez n'en fui,
> Fors que tant que mes euz en crui,
> Par cui sui en la voie entrez
> Donc ja n'istrai n'ainc n'en recrui.
>
> ('D'Amors, qui m'a tolu', 28-36)

(I never drank from the draft with which Tristan was poisoned; but my pure heart and noble intentions make me love
more than him. And I should be rewarded for this, for never
was I forced, except that I believed my eyes, because of which
I am set on the path that I will never leave nor renounce.)

Chrétien's position is diametrically opposed to Béroul's. Whereas
for Béroul the involuntary nature of Tristan and Yseult's love is what
makes it so powerful, here Chrétien explicitly says his love is wor-
thier because it owes nothing to any outside force. He believes his
eyes because they assure him of the beauty and qualities of his lady,
but he is at pains to portray his love as freely chosen. A true lover's
feelings, for Chrétien, cannot be attributed to a magic potion.

Chrétien obviously had strong feelings on the Tristan story,
since one of his romances – *Cligès* – seems to have been composed
as an anti-Tristan narrative. But it is characteristic of Chrétien's
light touch and deft sense of humour that his redeployment of elements of the Tristan story poses as many interpretative problems as
it resolves. The plot is complex and falls into two distinct halves:
first the story of a young Greek knight Alixandre, son of the
Emperor of Constantinople, and his love for Soredamors at King
Arthur's court; then that of their son Cligès and a Saxon princess,
Fenice. Inconveniently, Fenice is married to Cligès' uncle Alix,
who has usurped his throne: here then is the main ingredient of
the Tristan story. Because Fenice is keen to preserve her virginity
for the man she loves, she has her nurse prepare a magic potion
that will convince Alix he is having sex with her when he is in fact
hallucinating: this is but the first magic potion in the story, since
when Fenice and Cligès decide they cannot bear to go on with
Fenice married to his uncle, they have recourse to another potion
which enables Fenice to feign death, only to rise from the grave as
her name implied she would (Fenice = phoenix) to go and live in
secret with her lover in a tower, to which they soon add a garden.
When they are discovered the plot quickly unravels: they flee to
seek Arthur's help, but Alix conveniently dies before any war can
get going, so they become emperor and empress and live happily
ever after.

The family relations and magic potions are heavy hints that we should read *Cligès* intertextually against the Tristan story, but Chrétien does not stop there. The text opens with an explicit reference to a lost version of the *Tristan* by Chrétien himself:

> Cil qui fist d'Erec et d'Enide,
> Et les comandemenz d'Ovide
> Et l'art d'amors en romanz mist,
> Et le mors de l'espaule fist,
> Dou roi Marc et d'Iseult la Blonde,
> Et de la hupe de l'aronde
> Et du rousignol la muance,
> .I. novel conte recomence.
>
>   (*Cligès*, 1-8)

(The man who wrote *Erec et Enide* and Ovid's commandments and translated *The Art of Love* into French, and [who wrote] the *Bite on the Shoulder*, and the story of king Mark and Iseult the Blond, and of the hoopoe and the swallow, and about the nightingale's transformation, begins a new tale.)

The catalogue of his other works may not in itself be remarkable, though from this list only *Erec* survives: if Chrétien worked to commissions, it was probably important that his public knew which texts were his. What is more worthy of comment, if he did write a *Tristan*, is the way he refers to it: allusions to the story always use the hero's name, but Chrétien makes no mention of Tristan, instead drawing attention to the married, rather than the adulterous couple. Why should he refer to the story in this bizarre way?

The first two lovers – Alixandre and Soredamors – are sincere, but inept. The account of their inability to communicate their feelings to each other is comic, sometimes verging on the burlesque, as, for instance, when Alixandre writhes around in ecstasy all night clutching a shirt that has one of his beloved's hairs woven into it:

> Molt en fait toute la nuit grant joie
> Quant il est couchiez en son lit.

> A ce ou n'a point de delit
> Se delite en vain et soulace.
> Toute nuit la chemise enbrace,
> Et quant il le chevol remire,
> De tout le mont cuide estre sire.
> Bien fet Amors de sage fol
> Quant cil fet joie d'un chevol.

> (1626-34)

(He takes great joy from this all night when he is lying in his bed. He takes his pleasure and solace in vain where there is no pleasure to be had. He clutches the shirt all night and when he looks at the hair, he thinks himself the lord of the world. Love indeed makes a wise man into a fool when he gets joy from a hair.)

Chrétien's suggestive remark about Alixandre 'taking pleasure' with the shirt is followed up with overt ridicule. If he is sympathetic to the young lovers, he also jokes at their expense. It takes an intermediary (Guinevere) to get them together.

Chrétien's attitude towards the second generation of lovers is entirely different. Whereas his father had been a hesitant and interminably doubtful lover, Cligès is slick and confident, if not in the success of his suit, certainly in his feelings. He and Fenice cut to the chase all by themselves and make plans to get what they want. They are suave and able. Whereas Soredamors had been a timid and bashful maiden, Fenice seems to know all about sex and why she does not wish to have any with her husband: not only is she in love with his nephew, but if she were to conceive an heir for her husband this would effectively disinherit Cligès. She needs a potion and her nurse Thessala, who is usefully trained in medicinal arts, provides one. Fenice's motivation at this point is explicit. She does not wish to be like Yseult:

> Einz vodraie estre desmembree
> Que de nos .II. fust remembree
> L'amor d'Iseut et de Tristen,

Dont tantes folies dist l'en
Que hontes m'est a raconter.
Je ne me porroie acorder
A la vie qu'Ysez mena.
Amors en lui trop vilena,
Car li cors fu a dos rentiers
Et li cuers iere a un entiers.

(3099-108)

(I would rather be dismembered than have our love be
remembered as like that of Tristan and Yseult, about whom
so many foolish stories are told which I am ashamed to
repeat. I could never agree to live the life Yseult led. Love
grew too vile in her, for two men had a claim on her body
when her heart belonged to one alone.)

Again, when she asks for the second potion, which will enable her
to feign death, her explicit motivation is that she does not wish to
be like Yseult (5196-9). She does not wish her life to be used as a
negative moral example:

Ne ja nus par mon essamplaire
N'aprendra vilanie a faire.

(5187-8)

(No one, by my example, will learn to do bad things.)

And yet Fenice lies and cheats to get what she wants. Although Alix
is hardly a sympathetic character, given he effectively usurps
Cligès' throne, he is cruelly mocked, suffering the indignity of the
magic potion being served to him by none other than his nephew
and seeming totally ridiculous when he hallucinates having sex
with Fenice (see 3312-19). When the lovers are discovered in their
secret hide-out, our hero dismembers Bertrand, the unfortunate
knight who finds them, hardly a chivalrous act in that the text
implies his opponent, who has been hawking, is unarmed. If

Fenice's intention is to avoid Yseult's immorality, her attempt to do so leads her to questionable conduct.

This point is reinforced by *Cligès'* conclusion. Fenice and Cligès live happily ever after of course. They always trust each other and, unlike subsequent empresses of Contantinople, she is never again shut away from the world, as she was in the tower where she takes refuge after her feigned death:

> Qu'ainc puis n'i ot empereor
> N'eüst de sa feme peor
> Qu'ele nel deüst decevoir,
> Se il oï ramantevoir
> Comant Fenice Alis deçut
> Primes par la poison qu'il but
> Et puis par l'autre traïson.
> Por ce einsi com an prison
> Est gardee an Costantinoble,
> Ja n'iert tant riche ne tant noble
> L'empereriz, quex qu'ele soit,
> Que l'empereres ne la croit
> Tant com de cesti li remanbre.
> Toz jorz la fait garder en chanbre
> Plus por peor que por le hasle,
> Ne ja avoec li n'avra masle
> Qui ne soit chastrez en anfance,
> De ce n'est criemme ne dotance
> Qu'Amors les lit an son lien.
> Ci fenist l'uevre Crestien.

(6683-702)

(For never since then has there been an emperor who has not feared that his wife may deceive him when he hears the story of how Fenice deceived Alix, first with the potion that he drank and then with her other treachery. For this reason the empress of Constantinople, however rich and noble she may be, whoever she may be, is guarded as if she were in prison, for the emperor does not trust her as long as he remembers her predecessor. He always keeps her guarded in her chamber all the time out of fear rather than concern lest she be sun-burnt, nor is any male allowed to be with her, unless he has been castrated as a child so that there is no danger that love can bind them in its trap. Chrétien's work finishes here.)

The incongruity of this conclusion is frequently remarked upon by critics. Suddenly having this complex and deliciously comic text cast as an explanation of why the emperors of Constantinople keep their wives locked up comes as a surprise. Chrétien seems to have his tongue firmly in his cheek, but this mocking moral ending also reflects badly on Fenice: earlier in the text her main concern had been not to be remembered as a shameful figure, but the text concludes telling us that she was remembered primarily for her treachery and deception.

Characteristically, Chrétien has not written an 'anti-Tristan' in order to present us with a positive alternative model of love. Instead he uses subtle and intelligent humour to generate an intertextual dialogue that allows no firm conclusions. What this suggests is that he was working for a sophisticated and inquisitive literary public that was as interested in interpretation as it was in the subject matter. As with so many medieval texts, *Cligès* is designed not to offer an idealising presentation of courtly and chivalric values, but rather to elicit debate about these values.

Selected Reading

Chrétien de Troyes: *Cligès*, ed. Charles Méla and Olivier Collet (Paris, 1994). Includes the texts of the lyrics attributed to Chrétien.
Béroul and Thomas in *Tristan et Iseut: les poèmes français et la saga norroise*, ed. and trans. Daniel Lacroix and Philippe Walters (Paris, 1989).

Matilda Bruckner, *Shaping Romance* (see Chapter 3). Good chapter on Thomas.
Mark Chinca, *History, Fiction, Verisimilitude: Studies in the Poetics of Gottried's Tristan* (London, 1993). Many sections are relevant to Thomas.
Tony Hunt, 'Abelardian ethics and Béroul's *Tristan*', *Romania*, 98 (1977), 501-40. Explores responsibility, intention and sin.
—— 'The significance of Thomas's *Tristan*', *Reading Medieval Studies*, 7

(1981), 41-61. Persuasively argues that Thomas calls the morality of the lovers into question.

Michelle Freeman, 'Cligès', in *The Romances of Chrétien de Troyes: a Symposium*, ed. Douglas Kelly (Lexington, 1985), pp. 89-131. Good general study.

Sarah Kay, 'Courts, clerks and courtly love', in *The Cambridge Companion to Medieval Romance*, ed. Roberta L. Krueger (Cambridge 2000), pp. 81-96. Makes pertinent remarks about *Cligès* and the *Tristan* romances.

Toril Moi, '"She died because she came too late ...": knowledge, doubles and death in Thomas's *Tristan*', *Exemplaria*, 4 (1992), 105-33. Examines Thomas' complexity.

Lucie Polak, *Cligès* (London, 1982). Excellent general study, with a good section on the Tristan intertext.

See also the Selected Reading for Chapter 2.

Conclusion

Once and Future Stories

The proclivity for rewriting, continuation and interpretation that characterises medieval French literature ranges from the serious to the overtly comic. Furthermore, some medieval writers anticipate their texts being rewritten, continued, adapted. I shall conclude with an example from outside the period I have been examining, from the very end of the French Middle Ages: François Villon's *Testament* (fifteenth-century). In this fictional will, the testator-narrator adopts a range of registers, from the sublime to the obscene, to meditate upon death, love, poetry, and life. He leaves a considerable array of mock legacies to a long series of friends, family, enemies, and mere acquaintances. Some of his legacies are lyric poems, embedded in his longer poem: these, and literary references throughout, demonstrate an extensive knowledge of, and debt to, earlier literature, notably the *Roman de la Rose*, since it is evident that the character of *la belle heaumière* (an ageing former good-time girl) in the *Testament* owes a good deal to the *Rose*'s La Vieille. The *Testament* therefore absorbs and transforms other texts. Indeed it is, in any case, a reworking of an earlier fictional will, usually called the *Lais*, and to which Villon refers in order to revoke: any text is permanent only until it is rewritten. This seems to be the poet's point when he invites a reader to rewrite his own text:

> Pour ce que scet bien mon entente
> Jehan de Calaiz, honnorable homme,
> Qui ne me vist des ans a trente
> Et ne scet comment on me nomme,
> De tout ce testament en somme,

> S'aucun y a difficulté,
> L'oster jusque(es)' au rez d'une pomme
> Je lui en donne faculté.
>
> De le gloser et commanter,
> De le diffinir et descripre,
> Diminuer ou augmenter,
> De le canceller et prescripre
> De sa main – et ne sceut escripre –,
> Interpreter et donner sens
> A son plaisir, meilleur ou pire,
> A tout cecy je m'y consens.

$$(1844-59)$$

(Because he knows my intention, if anyone has any difficulty with it, I give permission to Jean de Calais, an honourable man who has not seen me these last thirty years and does not know my name, to cut this entire will and testament down until no more of it remains than the pip of an apple.

I allow him to do all this: to gloss and comment upon it, define and describe it, cut or expand it, tinker with it and cancel it with his own hand – even if he does not know how to write – interpret it and give it meaning as much as he likes, for better or worse.)

Typically, François Villon packs this request full of jokes. As the *Testament* opens by declaring the poet to be thirty years of age, line 1846 makes it clear Jean de Calais and Villon have never met, an implication reinforced by line 1847: it is hard, therefore, to see how Jean can have any sense of Villon's intentions. One might also wonder how Jean de Calais can undertake any revisions – with the possible exception of crossing out – to Villon's text if he is indeed illiterate (1856). But – on the cusp of the medieval and early modern periods – Villon seems to supply us with a description of medieval textuality: a text is not a fixed and stable entity; it is fluid, part of a process of rewriting and interpretation.

Roland Barthes concludes his influential essay 'The death of the author' with the remark that 'the birth of the reader must be at the cost of the death of the author' (p. 172), having argued that 'the text is a tissue of quotations drawn from innumerable centres of culture' (p. 170) and that 'a text's unity lies not in its origin but in its destination' (p. 171). He is seeking to displace a view of literature grounded largely in nineteenth- and twentieth-century realist fiction. According to this view, 'the Author is thought to *nourish* the book, which is to say that he exists before it, thinks, suffers, lives for it, is in the same relation of antecedence to his work as a father to his child' (p. 170). Barthes would prefer a view of the text 'made of multiple writings, drawn from many cultures and entering into mutual relations of dialogue, parody, contestation' (p. 171) and it is thus – implicitly – that he characterises modernity. For Barthes criticism has paid far too much attention to the author – and to his act of writing – and far too little to reading, which in his approach becomes a form of writing in that as a reader deciphers a text, s/he must effectively interpret and recreate it.

I hope that the relevance of these ideas to medieval literature are evident from the foregoing chapters. But Barthes' account only tells half the story since he fails to acknowledge that before the modern period far less restrictive views of authorship and textuality prevailed in Europe. Medieval writers acknowledge that texts do not derive exclusively from or belong to their authors, that they have multiple origins, that they are indeed 'a tissue of quotations' and, above all, that they go on developing and evolving as they are read, reread and rewritten in transmission. The invention of printing was ultimately to give the author some control over her or his text's future by fixing multiple copies, thereby diminishing the role of readers in transmission. As texts became the property of their authors, the role of the reader was thought by some to be limited to figuring out what the author intended. Barthes was reacting against what he saw as this reductive view of writing and reading. He wished to liberate modern writers and readers from this tyrannical view of the author, to liberate interpretation. But medieval writers and readers did not need liberating: they may, indeed, have had quite a lot in common with Barthes' ludic and subversive postmodern writers and readers. As Marie de France put it in her *Prologue* to the *Lais*, medieval writers and readers approached texts from the past in order to 'gloser la lettre/ et de lur sen le surplus metre' (16-17: to gloss their texts and add their own layer of wisdom). We, as readers of medieval texts today, are still free to join in and to enjoy this process.

Suggested Reading

François Villon: *Poésies complètes*, ed. Claude Thiry (Paris, 1991)

Roland Barthes, 'The death of the author', in *Modern Criticism and Theory: a Reader*, ed. David Lodge (London, 1988), pp. 167-72

Tony Hunt, *Villon's Last Will* (Oxford, 1996). Excellent general study, alert to the *Testament's* irony and play.

Douglas Kelly (ed.), *The Medieval Opus: Imitation, Rewriting, and Transmission in the French Tradition* (Amsterdam, 1996). Collection of essays on medieval textuality. The Introduction (pp. 1-11) offers an overview of the textual practices discussed in Chapters 4-7.

Glossary of Terms

For further information about these terms or about the authors or texts listed below, see Peter France (ed.), *The New Oxford Companion to Literature in French* (Oxford, 1995).

Anglo-Norman: dialect of French spoken in England by the ruling classes after 1066

chanson de geste: longer verse narrative devoted to the heroic deeds of knights (*geste* = 'legend' or 'deed'; also 'family'); generally set in the 8-10th centuries; written in *laisses*; the surviving 120 or so *chansons* are sometimes thought to belong to three distinct cycles: the *cycle du roi* (texts involving Charlemagne), the *cycle de Doon de Mayence* (texts about rebel barons, for example *Raoul de Cambrai*), and the cycle of William of Orange; most *chansons de geste* date from the period 1150-1250; they remain as popular as romance until prose romances become the dominant non-religious form of narrative in French speaking areas after about 1220

chevalerie: designates the ideal qualities attributed to knights

clergie: designates the skills of a clerk

compilation: the copying of different texts into a sequence in a single manuscript

cyclicity: the composition of texts that form part of a longer narrative, for example the *Prose Lancelot*, the *Prose Tristan*, the *Roman de Renart*, epics belonging to the cycle of William of Orange or about Roland

fabliaux: short comic narratives in octosyllabic rhyming couplets usually involving a trickster and a dupe, sometimes of a scabrous sexual nature

hagiography: narratives devoted to the life of a saint; often free translations of Latin texts; often extremely popular texts; saints' lives are usually written in octosyllabic rhyming couplets, but some early texts are written in *laisses* while some later texts use prose

lai: a short narrative in octosyllabic rhyming couplets using Celtic material; often with supernatural elements

laisses: stanzas of unequal length used as units of composition in *chansons de geste* and a few early saints' lives; usually decasyllabic (made up of lines of 10 syllables); either assonanced (the last vowel is the same throughout the *laisse*), or rhymed

laisses similaires: term used to designate a series of two or more *laisses* in which the action is repeated in similar terms; sometimes contrasted to *laisses parallèles*, in which different actions are narrated in similar terms in close sequence

matière de Bretagne: used to designate material that ostensibly has celtic sources

Occitan: language spoken in the Southern part of present-day France

octosyllabic rhyming couplets: 8-syllable lines rhyming in pairs

Prose romance: longer narrative texts that use material similar to that of earlier verse Arthurian romance, but written in prose; supersedes verse romance in popularity after about 1220, particularly the *Lancelot*

remaniement: the practice of recasting or rewriting existing textual material

roman antique: early romances drawing on earlier medieval Latin texts that transmit material from classical antiquity

romance: long narratives in octosyllabic rhyming couplets written after c.1150; romances also begin to be written in prose from the early 13th century; in addition to the *romans antiques*, Arthurian romances quickly appear and by the end of the 12th century romances are also set in the contemporary world; the main features of romance are often an interest in love and the foregrounding of a chivalric hero, but the genre also lends itself to historic narrative; verse romance and the *chanson de geste* are the dominant forms of non-religious narrative until about 1220

Main 12th and 13th-Century Authors writing in French

Those discussed in this book are given in bold.

Adam de la Halle: writer active in Arras in the 1260s and 70s; wrote lyrics, 2 plays (the *Jeu de la Feuillee* and the *Jeu de Robin et de Marion*), and an incomplete *chanson de geste*

Benoît de Sainte-Maure: author of the *Roman de Troie* (c.1160) and the incomplete *Chronique des Ducs de Normandie* (c.1175); worked at the court of Henry II, where he may have succeeded Wace as court chronicler

Béroul: author of a now fragmentary late 12th-c. *Roman de Tristan*

Bertrand de Bar-sur-Aube: one of the few named authors of a *chanson de geste*: wrote *Girart de Vienne* (late 12th-c.)

Chastelain de Coucy: well-known lyric poet (late 12th-c./early 13th-c.)

Chrétien de Troyes: author of five Arthurian romances written between c.1160 and c.1185: *Erec et Enide*, *Cligès*, *Yvain*, *Le Chevalier de la Charrete* (which was ostensibly finished by Godefroy de Lagny), *Le Conte du Graal* (which he left unfinished); there are also a few dense and allusive lyric poems attributed to him; may also have written a non-Arthurian romance, *Guillaume d'Angleterre*

Clemence of Barking: one of the few attested women writers in French from the Middle Ages, she was a nun in Barking and author of *La Vie de Sainte Catherine* (12th-c.)

Gace Brulé: prolific and gifted lyric poet (late 12th-c.) about whom very little is known

Gautier d'Arras: wrote a number of romances between c.1160 and c.1184 (*Eracle* and *Ille et Galeron*); these appear to have been well-known among contemporaries

Guillaume de Lorris: named by Jean de Meun as the author of the first part of the *Roman de la Rose*, which was probably written c.1225-40

Heldris de Cornualle: otherwise unknown author of the *Roman de Silence*, an extraordinary Arthurian romance about a girl brought up as a boy, probably written in the 1270s

Hue de Rotelande: important Anglo-Norman writer, author of *Ipomedon* (c.1180) and *Prothelaus* (c.1190)

Jean Bodel: prolific writer (d.1210) from Arras; author of *fabliaux*, a *chanson de geste*, and a play (*Le Jeu de saint Nicholas*) among other texts

Jean de Meun: probably the most important literary figure of the 13th c. (d.1305), Jean is best known for his continuation of the *Roman de la Rose*, but he also undertook a number of major translations from Latin and may have been the author of an early literary *Testament*

Jean Renart: early 13th-c.; witty and gifted author of the *Lai de l'ombre, Guillaume de Dole, L'Escoufle* and possible *Galeran de Bretagne*, probably the most original author of verse romance after Chrétien de Troyes

Marie de France: virtually nothing is known about Marie and she remains a shadowy figure; the Marie to whom the *Lais* are conventionally attributed was probably a French woman living in England during the reign of Henry II, who died in 1189; two other texts (the *Fables* and the *Espurgatoire saint Patrice*) are attributed to a 'Marie', who may or may not have been the same woman

Renaut de Beaujeu: author of the delightful late 12th-c. romance, *Le Bel Inconnu*

Robert de Blois: writer of didactic texts and a number of romances in the mid 13th c.

Robert de Boron: late 12th-c. author of three early grail romances

Robert de Clari: early 13th-c. writer from Picardy who wrote one of the earliest chronicles in French, *La Conquête de Constantinople*, some time after 1216, but about the Fourth Crusade in 1204

Rutebeuf: prolific, often humorous and idiosyncratic 13th-c. writer (c.1249-1277), who left some 56 texts in a wide variety of genres

Thomas of Britain: author of an important *Roman de Tristan* (c.1170) that now survives only in fragmentary form

Villehardouin, Geoffroi de: author of one of the earliest chronicles in French; like Robert de Clari, he wrote about the Fourth Crusade, though his *Conquête de Constantinople* was written earlier, in 1207

Wace: author of the *Brut* and the *Roman de Rou* as well as a number of saints' lives in the 1150s and 1160s, Wace worked at the court of Henry II; probably an influential figure in the evolution of early romance

Important Anonymous Texts in French from the 12th and 13th centuries

Those discussed in this book are given in bold.

Aliscans: chanson de geste from the cycle of William of Orange (c.1170)

Ami et Amile: chanson de geste (c.1200) the plot of which is also used for a saint's life and a romance; has Latin sources and is adapted into English

Charroi de Nîmes: chanson de geste from the cycle of William of Orange (c.1150)

Chanson de Guillaume: early (c.1100) *chanson de geste* telling part of the story of William of Orange, later retold in *Aliscans*; continued and revised c.1150

Chanson de Roland: *chanson de geste* that was rewritten repeatedly throughout the 12th century

Chastelaine de Vergi: remarkable 13th-c. short romance, telling the story of the ill-fated Chastelaine, whose secret love is betrayed by her suitor; a popular and influential tale

Couronnement de Louis: chanson de geste from the cycle of William of Orange (1130s or 40s)

Floire et Blancheflor: early verse romance (c.1150) that was rewritten and translated into English

Lancelot: prose romance (c.1215) that may or may not have been conceived as a separate text before becoming part of a larger cycle including the *Queste* and the *Mort*

Mort le roi Artu: attributed implausibly to Walter Map, part of the *Lancelot* cycle (c.1230)

Queste del saint Graal: attributed implausibly to Walter Map, part of the *Lancelot* cycle (c.1230)

Prise d'Orange: chanson de geste from the cycle of William of Orange (c.1190)

Raoul de Cambrai: magnificent *chanson de geste*, narrating Raoul's rebellion against his king and the ensuing blood-curdling family feud (c.1190); the surviving version is the result of *remaniement* and continuation

Roman de Renart: collection of some 26 short narratives about Renart the

fox and other members of the animal kingdom, composed between
c.1170 and c.1250

Roman d'Eneas: influential *roman antique* based on Virgil (c.1160)

Roman de Thèbes: *roman antique* (c.1160)

Vie de Saint Alexis: early saint's life (11th-c.) that is subsequently rewritten

Vie de Sainte Marie l'Egyptienne: popular saint's life that is rewritten repeatedly

Chronological Table

This table provides only a few key historical events alongside approximate dates of the texts discussed in the course of this book. Because the dating of early medieval texts is so difficult, I have only attempted to assign texts to a decade, and even here some doubts must remain. The table does not give dates for all surviving French texts from the period.

	Historical events	Literary texts; approximate dates
1050		*Vie de Saint Alexis*
1060	Battle of Hastings (1066)	
1070		
1080		
1090	First Crusade (1095-99)	
1100	Henry I, King of England	Oxford *Roland*
1100	Louis VI, King of France (1108)	
1110		
1120		
1130	Louis VII, King of France (1137)	Geoffrey of Monmouth, *Historia*
1140	Second Crusade (1147-50)	*Couronnement de Louis*
1150	Louis VII divorces Eleanor of Aquitaine (1152) Henry II, King of England (1154)	Wace, *Roman de Brut*; *Roman d'Eneas*
1160		Benoît de Sainte-Maure, *Roman de Troie*; Wace, *Roman de Rou*; Chrétien de Troyes, *Erec et Enide*
1170	Thomas Beckett murdered	Béroul, *Tristan* (?); Chrétien, *Cligès, Yvain, Charrete*; Thomas, *Tristan*; Marie de France, *Lais*; *Roman de Renart* begins
1180	Philippe-Auguste, King of France (1180) Richard II, King of England (1189)	Chrétien, *Le Conte du Graal*; *Roman de Renart* continues; T version of *La Vie de Saint Marie l'Egyptienne* (?)
1190	Third Crusade (1191) John Lackland, King of England (1199)	First continuation of *Le Conte du Graal*; Paris *Roland* (?); *Raoul de Cambrai* (?)
1200	Fourth Crusade (1202)	
1210		Prose *Lancelot* (?)
1220	Louis VIII, King of France (1223) Louis IX, King of France (1226)	
1230		*Queste* and *Mort* (?); Guillaume de Lorris, *Roman de la Rose*
1240		
1250		
1260		Rutebeuf, *Vie de Sainte Marie l'Egyptienne*
1270	Philip III, King of France (1270)	Jean de Meun, *Roman de la Rose*
1280	Philip the Fair, King of France (1285)	
1290		

Index of Critics

General Index